The Deeper Journey

The Spirituality Of Discovering Your True Self

M. Robert Mulholland Jr.

16pt

Read How You Want
LARGE PRINT BOOKS, BRAILLE & DAISY

Copyright Page from the Original Book

InterVarsity Press
P.O. Box 1400, Downers Grove, IL 60515-1426
ivpress.com
email@ivpress.com

InterVarsity Press® is the book-publishing division of InterVarsity Christian Fellowship/USA®, a movement of students and faculty active on campus at hundreds of universities, colleges and schools of nursing in the United States of America, and a member movement of the International Fellowship of Evangelical Students. For information about local and regional activities, visit intervarsity.org.

All Scripture quotations, unless otherwise indicated, are the author's own translation.

While any stories in this book are true, some names and identifying information may have been changed to protect the privacy of individuals.

Cover design: Cindy Kiple
Interior design: Beth McGill
Images: © pauloribau / iStockphoto

ISBN 978-0-8308-4618-4 (print)
ISBN 978-0-8308-9374-4 (digital)

Printed in the United States of America ∞

Library of Congress Cataloging-in-Publication Data

Names: Mulholland, M. Robert, Jr., author.
Title: The deeper journey : the spirituality of discovering your true self /
  M. Robert Mulholland Jr.
Description: Expanded Edition. | Downers Grove : InterVarsity Press, 2016. |
  Includes bibliographical references.
Identifiers: LCCN 2015050889 (print) | LCCN 2016001993 (ebook) | ISBN
  9780830846184 (pbk. : alk. paper) | ISBN 9780830893744 (eBook)
Subjects: LCSH: Self-perception—Religious aspects—Christianity.
Classification: LCC BV4598.25 .M85 2016 (print) | LCC BV4598.25 (ebook) | DDC
  248.4—dc23
LC record available at http://lccn.loc.gov/2015050889

P	20	19	18	17	16	15	14	13	12	11	10	9	8	7	6	5	4	3	2	1
Y	33	32	31	30	29	28	27	26	25	24	23	22	21	20	19	18	17	16

TABLE OF CONTENTS

"Most of us are aware that there is something that is not quite right within us. When we are honest, we might even admit that there is something terribly wrong. It is called the false self. *The Deeper Journey* provides understanding and guidance for the journey from the false self to the true self. It is a harrowing journey, to be sure, but it is also a journey of hope and healing and freedom. This book is full of much-needed wisdom from one of the most trusted spiritual guides of our time."

RUTH HALEY BARTON, COFOUNDER OF THE TRANSFORMING CENTER, AND AUTHOR OF *SACRED RHYTHMS* AND *LIFE TOGETHER IN CHRIST*

"Dr. Mulholland's exposition of the transforming journey from the noxious web of the false self to the liberating reality of the true self is totally compelling and a must-read for disciples serious about the 'with-God' life."

BRUCE DEMAREST, PROFESSOR OF CHRISTIAN FORMATION, DENVER SEMINARY

"What a wonderfully mending and unsettling read. I read it and started reading it all over again. Mulholland serves as an experienced guide to what it means to have an inner life, a life that is 'hidden with Christ in God.' His voice helps me attend to the well-defended and self-referenced way I do life—even my spiritual life. The Deeper Journey is rich with the practical implications of what it means to be 'in God for the world.'"

ADELE CALHOUN, AUTHOR, *SPIRITUAL DISCIPLINES HANDBOOK*

"Mulholland recommends radical honesty about ourselves as an essential part of the foundation of a deeper faith. We Christians in North America definitely need to ponder his conviction that the false self and the religious false self will lead us on dead-end roads. I found Mulholland's invitation to a deeper journey in Christ to be profoundly challenging and winsomely encouraging."

LYNNE M. BAAB, AUTHOR OF *SABBATH KEEPING* AND *BEATING BURNOUT IN CONGREGATIONS*

"Carrying the journey beyond that introduced in his earlier

much-appreciated *Invitation to a Journey,* this new book by Robert Mulholland will be very helpful to all those who feel called to a deeper journey and who wonder how concepts such as the true and false self relate to biblical teaching. If this is you, read on and be prepared to meet God and yourself more deeply."

DAVID G. BENNER, DISTINGUISHED PROFESSOR OF PSYCHOLOGY AND SPIRITUALITY, PSYCHOLOGICAL STUDIES INSTITUTE, AND AUTHOR OF *THE GIFT OF BEING YOURSELF*

Formatio books from InterVarsity Press follow the rich tradition of the church in the journey of spiritual formation. These books are not merely about being informed, but about being transformed by Christ and conformed to his image. Formatio stands in InterVarsity Press's evangelical publishing tradition by integrating God's Word with spiritual practice and by prompting readers to move from inward change to outward witness. InterVarsity Press uses the chambered nautilus for Formatio, a symbol of spiritual formation because of its continual spiral journey outward as it moves from its center. We believe that each of us is made with a deep desire to be in God's presence. Formatio books help us to fulfill our deepest desires and to become our true selves in light of God's grace.

For Lynn,
beloved companion on the journey

ACKNOWLEDGMENTS

My deep thanks to Dr. Maxie Dunnam, former president of Asbury Theological Seminary, and to the board of trustees who graciously provided a year of sabbatical leave for me to develop this sequel to *Invitation to a Journey*. I am also grateful to my colleagues, to my students and to innumerable gatherings of earnest seekers of the deeper journey, with whom the insights of this book were nurtured. I am indebted to Al Hsu, my editor at InterVarsity Press, and all his colleagues whose diligent labors were invaluable in polishing this work (any "rough spots" are my responsibility).

Above all, I can never adequately acknowledge the profound role of my wife, Lynn, who proofread numerous iterations of the manuscript; sat through even more numerous classes, seminars and retreats where this material took shape; and provided valuable feedback and insights. Without her love, encouragement and support this book would be far, far less.

1

THE GOAL

Gracious and loving God, in love you spoke me into being before the foundation of the world. Your love has enfolded and indwelled me through all the winding paths of my life, and your love has prepared me for this book. Help me so to open myself to your indwelling love that this book may be a place of transforming encounter with you. Amen.

I suspect you are reading this book because the idea of a "deeper journey" touched a chord within you. You may have been on the Christian journey for some time or perhaps you are a newcomer to life in Christ. Whichever the case, you may have reached a point in your walk with God where your relationship with God has become somewhat stale. The things that excited and stimulated you at the first stages of your journey have become routine.

You hunger for a deeper, richer, fuller life with God.

Once I asked the pastor of a large, vigorous, dynamic, growing church with a strong emphasis on the deeper life in Christ—and a church that confirmed fifty to seventy-five new members each week—where these people were coming from. His response surprised me. He told me that almost all of these people had begun their journey in Christ in an even larger, more vigorous, more dynamic church whose worship was leading-edge contemporary, whose focus was strongly charismatic and whose corporate life centered in highly emotional expressions of faith in God. These people would stay in this church for about two to three years and then the novelty and excitement would become ritualized and dry for them. They began to hunger, in his words, "for something deeper." They began to sense that there was more to the Christian life.

You may have asked yourself, *Isn't there more to the Christian life than being active in a Christian community, affirming a certain set of beliefs, adopting a particular behavior pattern?* You may have wondered about the purpose of the Christian life. As you probably know well, this line of questions brings forth a multitude of answers. This multiplicity itself reveals a great lack of clarity on the nature of the Christian life.

The biblical answer to the question is: To be like Jesus. You may be thinking that this is pretty ambiguous, and given the diversity of ideas of what being like Jesus entails, you would be right. For instance, is the recent fad of "What Would Jesus Do?" with its jewelry, clothing, Bible covers and bracelets the way to be like Jesus? Or is there much more to it than this? Just what does it mean to be like Jesus? Let's investigate some of the biblical indicators.

If the purpose of the Christian life is to be like Jesus, it might be a good idea to first get some idea of who Jesus is. Paul describes Jesus in this way: "In him all the fullness of God was pleased to dwell" (Col 1:19 NRSV). I doubt that you have difficulty with this idea. The Word, which is God, became flesh in

Jesus (Jn 1:1, 14). You may also remember some of Paul's other affirmations such as "God was in Christ" (2 Cor 5:19) and "Christ, who is the image of God" (2 Cor 4:4 NRSV). Jesus himself said, "The one who has seen me has seen the Father" (Jn 14:9), "I and the Father are one" (Jn 10:30) and "The Father is in me and I am in the Father" (Jn 10:38 NRSV). The writer of Hebrews tells us Jesus is "the reflection of God's glory and the exact imprint of God's very being" (Heb 1:3 NRSV). So when Paul tells us that all the fullness of God was in Jesus, he is simply summarizing what these and other New Testament passages convey—God and Jesus are in a profound and mysterious union with each other.

Now here is something remarkable. Alongside Paul's claim that all the fullness of God was pleased to dwell in Christ, have you ever noticed Paul's prayer for believers in Ephesians 3:19? Paul prays "that you may be filled with all the fullness of God" (NRSV)! Paul seems to be praying that we would be like Jesus! We are to have something of the same profound and mysterious union with God that Jesus has as the revelation of our true humanness in the image of God.

Paul demonstrates this amazing perspective for us in a number of ways. "Speaking the truth in love, we must grow up in every way into him who is the head, into Christ" (Eph 4:15 NRSV). Two verses earlier Paul writes that we are all to achieve "maturity, ... the measure of the full stature of Christ" (NRSV). Paul tells the Corinthians that we, "beholding the glory of the Lord, are being changed into his likeness" (2 Cor 3:18), and he urges the Philippians to have the same way of being that Jesus had (Phil 2:5-8).

We should note, however, Paul is not alone in this understanding of the purpose of the Christian life being Christlikeness. Peter, after telling us that God has called us to his own glory,[1] writes that God has given us "his precious and very great promises, so that through them you may escape from the corruption that is in the world because of lust, and may become participants of the divine nature" (2 Pet 1:4 NRSV). John says, "When he is revealed, we will be like him, for we will see him as he is" (1 Jn 3:2 NRSV).

You would be wise to ask at this point, where do these men get this outlandish idea that we are to be like Jesus? I suspect that its origins lie with Jesus himself. Look at this radical statement of what the Christian life is all about in Jesus' prayer in John 17:

> I ask not only on behalf of these [the eleven disciples], but also on behalf of those who will believe in me through their word [that is us!], that they may all be one. As you, Father, are in me and I am in you, may they also be in us, so that the world may believe that you have sent me. The glory that you have given me I have given them, so that they may be one, as we are one, I in them and you in me, that they may become completely one, so that the world may know that you have sent me and have loved them even as you have loved me. (Jn 17:20-23 NRSV)

We should note that when Jesus prays that we may all be one, he is not praying for some kind of sociological or theological or ecclesiological or liturgical unity. He is not asking for a homogeneity that levels all diversity and brings plurality into a single "authorized" manifestation of the Christian life or community. The unity, the oneness Jesus prays for, is illustrated by his own relationship with God: "As you, Father, are in me and I am in you, may they also be in us." Jesus is praying that you and I would live in a similar kind of relationship with God that he has as the revelation of true humanness in the image of God. Jesus is indicating that the purpose of the Christian life is a life of loving union with God at the depths of our being.

We see the profound nature of Jesus' prayer when he says, "The glory that you have given me I have given them, so that they may be one, as we are one." To understand what is going on here we need to have a little lesson in Greek. (Don't worry, it won't hurt.) "Glory" is the translation of a Greek word that represents the essential characteristics or nature of a person or thing that makes them who they are.

Thus the "glory" of God is God's very nature, the essence of who God is.

Let's look at some places in the New Testament where this meaning of "glory" opens up a verse to much deeper dimensions. For instance, Peter writes, "the spirit of glory, which is the Spirit of God, is resting on you" (1 Pet 4:14 NRSV). Note that in the parallelism of the text, glory = God. Peter also says that we have been called to God's "glory" (1 Pet 5:10), that is, to be partakers of God's own nature (2 Pet 1:3-4). Paul indicates that as a result of our sin, we have fallen short of the "glory" of God (Rom 3:23), but now that we have been restored in our relationship with God through Christ, we hope to share the "glory" of God (Rom 5:2).

Do you remember the passage we looked at a few pages back, "We all, ... beholding the glory of the Lord, are being changed into his likeness" (2 Cor 3:18)? Here again, the parallelism of the passage reveals that glory = "likeness." The rest of the verse is "from glory into glory." When Paul says we are being changed from glory into glory, he means that we are being changed from what we are in our unlikeness to Christ into his likeness. All this suggests that when Jesus says that he has given to us the "glory" that God has given to him, he is indicating that he has made it possible for us to once again be formed in the image of God, to share God's nature as we were intended. Jesus is saying that he has imparted to us God's nature that dwells in him. He has made possible the restoration of union with God.

At this point we might be tempted to think that this union with God is a private "possession" for our individual benefit. Jesus disabuses us of this temptation. He indicates there is yet a larger purpose for our union with God: "That the world may believe.... [S]o that the world may know that you have sent me" (Jn 17:21, 23 NRSV). Union with God results in our being a person through whom God's presence touches the world with forgiving, cleansing, healing, liberating and transforming grace. John saw this clearly: "As he is, so are we in this world" (1 Jn 4:17 NRSV). The world will not believe in

Christ because of our sound theology, our correct creed, our well defined dogma, our rigorous religiosity. The world will believe when it sees Christlikeness manifested in our life. The world will know that God has sent Christ not simply because we pronounce it to be so but when they see Christlikeness lived out in their midst in our lives in the world.

Such Christlikeness, however, is the consequence of a loving union with God. This is why Jesus finishes his prayer for us with the words "that the world may know that you ... have loved them even as you have loved me" (Jn 17:23 NRSV). The source of a loving union with God lies in God's unfathomable love for us. Think of it—Jesus says that God loves you in exactly the same way that God loves him! To respond to such love with the love of your total being draws you into that loving union with God for which Jesus prays.

To be like Jesus, then, as it is portrayed in the New Testament, is a matter of both "being" and "doing." It is being in a relationship of loving union with God that manifests itself in Christlike living in the world.

It is to this life of deep, loving union with God that the mothers and fathers of our spiritual tradition call us. Let's look at a few examples from across the centuries. Archbishop Demetrios, writing of Ignatius of Antioch, one of the earliest church fathers (late first to early second century), says, "The absolute priority of God, *the vital need for a real, existential connection with Him,* the urgency of focusing on Him *and entering into an advanced, total relationship with Him,* seems to be the Ignatian message reaching our present."[2] We can see here that the second generation of believers had entered into the loving union with God that Jesus, Paul, Peter and John described.

A couple of centuries later Athanasius of Alexandria wrote, "He became man that we might be made god."[3] Now you might think this is a rather bold and extreme affirmation, and it certainly is. But isn't this simply another way to express Peter's contention that we are to become partakers of the divine nature (2 Pet 1:4)?

I suspect you might be thinking at this point that all this seems rather theoretical and esoteric. So let's look at some testimonies of people who have experienced this loving union with God. Simeon the New Theologian (A.D.949-1022) describes in third person his experience of union with God:

> A divine radiance suddenly appeared in abundance from above and filled the whole room. When this happened, the young man lost all awareness of his surroundings and forgot whether he was in a house or under a roof. He saw nothing but light on every side, and did not even know if he was standing on the ground.... He was wholly united to non-material light and, so it seemed, he had himself been turned into light.[4]

This is, of course, an ecstatic instance of profound union with God and not a normal everyday experience. You might liken it to those moments of ecstatic union in a marriage relationship (and the mothers and fathers of our spiritual tradition often use marriage as an analogy for our relationship with God). Such moments are not the norm of the marriage relationship, but they can serve to bond the couple ever deeper in their love for one another. As a couple's love relationship grows and deepens, their union begins to become the primary context of their life in the world.

Here is another example using the image of light. Gregory Palamas (d. 1359) writes: "Participating in that light which surpasses them they are themselves transformed into it.... [T]he light alone shines through them and it alone is what they see ... and in this way God is all in all."[5] I heard or read once a famous conductor's experience in leading a world-class orchestra in a performance of a great composer's masterpiece. On this occasion the orchestra became so united with the music that the conductor simply stopped leading them and stood and listened in awe as the orchestra became the incarnation of the composer's masterpiece. Writing of Francis of Assisi, Bonaventura (d.

A.D.1274) said, "He seemed to be totally absorbed in the flame of divine love ... and he longed to be totally transformed into him [Christ] by the fire of ecstatic love."[6] You say, "But these are the great saints of our tradition." True, but aren't they the illustrations of what we are all created to become? After all, if Jesus prayed for you that you might have the same loving union with God that he has, should you be surprised that some of our sisters and brothers in the faith have actually lived in this reality?

Let's pick up the marriage image again. In his *Spiritual Canticle,* John of the Cross (A.D.1542-1591) focuses on the soul's "espousal" and union with God: "Love never reaches perfection until the lovers are so alike that one is transfigured in the other."[7] He then amplifies this:

> This spiritual marriage is incomparably greater than the spiritual espousal, for it is a total transformation in the beloved in which each surrenders the entire possession of the self to the other with a certain consummation of the

union of love. The soul thereby becomes divine, becomes God through participation, insofar as is possible in this life.... It is accordingly the highest state attainable in this life.[8]

Also speaking of this spiritual marriage—the union of the soul with God—John's spiritual director, Teresa of Ávila (A.D.1515-1582) writes: "One can say no more—insofar as can be understood—than that the soul, I mean the spirit, is made one with God."[9]

I hope you are beginning to see that the Christian life in its fullness is far more than being active in a Christian community, affirming a certain set of beliefs or adopting a particular behavior pattern. These are a secondary result of the primary reality of a life engaged in an ever deepening union with God in love.

Kallistos Ware puts it like this, "Christianity is not merely a philosophical theory or a moral code, but involves a direct sharing in divine life and glory, a transforming union with God 'face to face.'" [10] One of the ways in which this sharing in divine life restructures our journey is a decentering of our experience of prayer. Writing of the prayer of the heart in the Eastern tradition, Ware says, " 'Prayer of the heart,' therefore, means not just 'affective prayer' but *prayer of the entire person.... [A] state of reintegration, in which the one who prays is totally united with the prayer itself and with the Divine Companion to whom the prayer is addressed.* "[11] Prayer itself becomes the experience of loving union with God. Doesn't this provide you with a whole new perspective on Paul's injunction to "pray without ceasing" (1 Thess 5:17 NRSV)?

Finally, let me conclude this brief historical excursion of life in loving union with God with the insight of Thomas Merton (A.D.1915-1968): "This Spirit of God, dwelling in us, given to us, to be as it were our own Spirit, enables us to know and experience, in a mysterious manner, the reality and presence of the divine mercy in ourselves. So the Holy Spirit is intimately united to our own inmost self, and His presence in us makes our 'I' the 'I' of God."[12] This is but a small sample of the theme of union with God in love that runs strong and deep through two millennia of Christian life and experience. It is to this reality that I hope to introduce you in the chapters that follow.

If you already live in this loving union with God, if every thought, word and deed flow forth from this divine center of love in your life, then read no farther. But if something deep within you hungers and thirsts for this reality, if the idea of loving union with God stirs an awakening in the depths of your being, then read on. It is the basic premise of this book that loving union with God is the essence of the Christian life in the world. I should warn you, however, that the deeper journey into this loving union with God passes through some pretty rough territory—the jungle of the false self (chap. 2) and the world of the idol and its box, the religious false self (chap. 3)—before we come to the borders of the country of the Christ self (chap. 4) and enter into its twofold rhythm of wholeness: putting off the vices (chap. 5) and putting on the virtues (chap. 6). Finally, I must echo, even more fully than he, the caveat of John of the Cross: "Everything I say is as far from the reality as is a painting from the living object represented."[13] While a painting may be accurate to the last detail, only those who live in the reality it represents know that reality as the life of their being. It is my hope that God will enable my "painting" to become for you a transforming encounter with the reality of which my "painting" is but a pale, poor shadow.

2

INTO THE JUNGLE

The False Self

Gracious and loving God, I give you praise and thanks for the ways in which you have met me and touched me and nurtured me through the years of my life. I thank you for weaving this book into my life. As I ponder these things, help me to offer myself to you that you may be in me all that you want to be. Help me to keep myself abandoned to you in love that you may have your way with me. I ask this in Jesus' name. Amen.

One of the things I suspect you may have discovered on your pilgrimage is that consciously or unconsciously you bring to a book the current context of your spiritual journey. We open the book with some pretty clear ideas of what we want, what we hope to experience, what we expect to receive.

We bring our own agenda to the table, so to speak.

I hope, however, at this point in your spiritual journey you've discovered there is always a deeper agenda at work in your life. God has an agenda for you. God's agenda catches up the threads of your agenda, weaving these together in ways radically different than you expected.

So I would urge you as we share this book together to make yourself available to God and give God permission to do whatever God wants to do in your life through this book.

TWO WAYS OF BEING IN THE WORLD

Jeremiah writes:
Thus says the LORD:
Cursed are those who trust in mere mortals and make mere flesh their strength, whose hearts turn away from the LORD.
They shall be like a shrub in the desert, and shall not see when relief comes.

They shall live in the parched
places of the wilderness, in an
uninhabited salt land.

Blessed are those who trust in the
LORD, whose trust is the LORD.
They shall be like a tree planted
by water, sending out its roots by
the stream.
It shall not fear when heat comes,
and its leaves shall stay green;
in the year of drought it is not
anxious, and it does not cease to
bear fruit.

The heart is devious above all else;
it is perverse—
who can understand it?
I the LORD test the mind
and search the heart. (Jer 17:5-10
NRSV)

In a very focused way Jeremiah
illuminates a reality that threads its way
from Genesis through Revelation. He
reveals there are two fundamental ways
of being human in the world: trusting
in our human resources and abilities or
a radical trust in God. You cannot be

grasped by or sustained in the deeper life in God—being like Jesus—until you are awakened at the deep levels of your being to this essential reality. You might describe these two ways of being in the world as the "false self" and the "true self."[1]

I will never forget the experience that awakened me to this reality. As a fairly young Christian I thought of repentance for my sins in terms of being sorry for things I had done. I was really, sincerely sorry, yet kept doing the same things over and over again. You may have been there yourself. Then I heard a wise teacher say, "Repentance is not being sorry for the things you have done, but being sorry you are the kind of person that does such things." With that I began the disturbing discovery of my false self. I began to realize that underneath the thin veneer of my religiosity lived a pervasive and deeply entrenched self-referenced being which was driven by its own agendas, its own desires, its own purposes,[2] and that no amount of superficial tinkering with the religious façade made any appreciable difference.

Then I happened to read those familiar words: "If we confess our sins, he is faithful and just so that he might forgive us our sins and might cleanse us from all unrighteousness" (1 Jn 1:9). This time the words exploded in my mind and heart. I realized for the first time that God's purpose for us was not simply to forgive sins but to transform our false self—to cleanse all its unrighteousness, to make us righteous, to restore us to our true self in loving relationship with God and in being Christlike in the world. I realized that the false self I was stood in the way of becoming the true self for which I had been created. I was a mud pie with a thin layer of Christian frosting trying to pass myself off as an angel food cake, but the mud kept seeping through! I needed God to take that mud and breathe into it the breath of life.

Unless you are aware of these two selves, these two ways of being in the world, you will have great difficulty allowing God to lead you into a deeper life of wholeness in Christ. Let's first unpack together some of the crucial dynamics of the false self. Then we'll unpack the dynamics of the true self. Once we have done this, we can then begin to explore the dynamics of the deeper life in God.

THE FALSE SELF

Let us begin to get our minds and our hearts around an understanding of the false self.[3] Perhaps a rather embarrassing personal example will help to set the stage for our thinking.

A personal example. Have you ever had a Romans 7 moment, one similar to what Paul describes when he says, "The good I want to do, I don't do; the evil I don't want to do, is what I do" (Rom 7:19)? I suspect you have had some of those moments. I had such a moment recently.

Now, my false self, like most false selves, is a control freak that manipulates people and situations to protect it from disturbances to its status quo. I had returned to my office one Tuesday morning after being away for a day and found a note indicating that the first leg of my Sunday flight from Lexington, Kentucky, to Dubuque, Iowa, for an upcoming speaking engagement had been canceled. What a great way to start the day! I called the airline and, sure enough, they had canceled the flight. When I asked why, I was told, "No equipment." Hey, wait a minute folks. This was Tuesday. No equipment five days from now? I mean, shift something around, get a plane there!

Well, we finally worked it out. At first they tried to fly me to Charlotte, North Carolina, then to Chicago and on to Dubuque. I said, "You can do better than that." They finally got me on another airline from Lexington to Detroit to Chicago and then put me back with the original airline for the flight to Dubuque. I called my travel agent, he printed out the tickets, and my wife picked them up.

My agent told me, "I checked it through and everything's in order. All you need to do is take the tickets to the desk of the airline you are flying."

When I arrived at the airport on Sunday, I took my tickets to the desk of the airline I was flying.

The agent looked at my tickets and said, "You have to go down to the original airline with these."

"Well, that's not what I was told," I retorted.

My false self was beginning to exercise itself. It didn't want to be out of control. After all, I had taken great steps to make sure that this wasn't going to happen! So I stormed down to the original airline (well, I wasn't quite "storming" yet, but I was certainly building up a head of steam!). I told the agent that he needed to put some notification on my ticket indicating the change from his airline to the other. The agent proceeded to write on the first ticket—the original but now-canceled flight to Chicago—and then he began to write on the ticket from Chicago to Dubuque.

Exasperated, I said, "No, no, no; I'm still on that one. That's my flight from Chicago to Dubuque on your airline. It's just from here to Chicago that I need the help."

The agent got on the computer, typed a while and then said, "No, we don't have you going from Chicago to

Dubuque, not on our airline. You must be on the other airline."

Well, the other agent had already told me they only had me to Chicago. So now I could get to Chicago, but not to Dubuque, in spite of all my carefully controlled plans.

I told the agent, even more forcefully, "No, wait a minute, I'm supposed to be on your flight to Dubuque."

"Well," he said, "You're not listed here."

Now I was really getting steamed. I went storming back to the first airline and after much heated dialogue with the agent, we finally got it all settled and I got my flight from Chicago to Dubuque on the original airline.

These, however, were only the preliminaries. When I got to the security check they had a sign: "If you have a computer take it out and put it on the belt." Now I carry my computer, in its case, in my larger carry-on case. So I set my carry-on case down and, as I have done every time for years, opened it up, pulled out my computer in its computer case and put it on the conveyer, and then put my carry-on case on the conveyer and went through the metal detector.

When I got to the other side of the conveyer, the lady asked me, "Is this a computer?"

"Yes," I said.

"Well, you have to take it out of the case," she replied.

With that, I just lost it. That was the end. I snarled, "What do you mean I have to take it out of the case?"

She retorted firmly, "You have to take it out of the case and put it through separately. The sign says so."

"I come through here all the time," I ranted. "I've never had to take this out of the case."

"Well, you have to take it out of the case," she said, becoming rather agitated herself.

I practically screamed, "I was through here last Friday and I put it through and didn't have to take it out of the case."

"You've got to take it out of the case," she yelled.

I snatched the computer from her, stormed back through the metal detector, took the computer from its case, slammed the case on the conveyer, put the computer through and stormed back through the metal detector, completely oblivious to the people I was inconveniencing by my tirade. You see, my false self went into high gear because it wasn't able to be in control. All my careful manipulations had failed; all the steps I had taken to protect myself from something like this had been worthless.

I have found the term "false self" very helpful to describe what was behind the attitude and behavior I exhibited on this occasion. I was a thoroughly self-referenced being.

THE FALSE SELF IN THE BIBLICAL STORY

The false self appears early in the biblical story. We see the essence of this false self in the original temptation. The tempter says, "If you eat this fruit, you will be like God" (Gen 3:5). The temptation to take over God's role in our life is the essence of the false self. The false self is a self that in some way is playing god in its life and in its world. I will unpack various aspects of this false self in what follows.

You are created to experience your true life, your genuine identity, your deepest meaning, your fullest purpose, your ultimate value in an intimate, loving union with God at the core of your being. As we saw in the previous chapter, the depths of this union are made clear in Jesus' amazing prayer for us in John 17:20-23. The oneness Jesus prays for us to experience is a union with God that is the same as his union with God in his revelation as true humanness in the image of God. ("As you, Father, are in me and I am in you ... that they may be one, as we are one.") We also saw Paul indicating that we are to be like Jesus in our relationship with God. In fact, Paul tells the Colossians, "Your life is hidden with Christ in God" (Col 3:3 NRSV). When we play god in our lives, this union is lost. We become autonomous, self-referenced beings who have abandoned the center of our true identity in God. We objectify or identify our self apart from God.

This reality is powerfully imaged early in the biblical story. Even after Cain murders his brother Abel (Gen 4:1-8), he still has a "face to face" relationship with God (Gen 4:9-15). But then we are told: "Cain went away from the presence of the LORD, and settled in the land of Nod, east of Eden" (Gen 4:16 NRSV). Notice God did not abandon Cain. Cain turned his back on God. The result was a radical decentering of Cain's life. He finds himself in a land of wandering—the Hebrew term *Nod* means "wandering." Cain finds himself in a mode of being that has no firm center of identity, no solid foundation of meaning, no bedrock ground of value, no root of purpose.

The next thing Cain does in the story is "build for himself a city" (Gen 4:17). You see, it was necessary for Cain to create for himself a structure that would provide a center of identity, meaning, value and purpose to replace the center he lost when he pulled the roots of his being out of God. You find the amplification of this story in the account of Babel (Gen 11:1-9). Here, people from the east—the place where

Cain went, "the land of Nod, *east* of Eden"—build a city for themselves. Like Cain, they are attempting to create for themselves a structure of life that will provide a center of identity. They had realized that the alternative was a decentered existence—"scattered abroad upon the face of the whole earth." Interestingly, in their self-generated structure for life, they create "a tower with its top in the heavens" (Gen 11:4 NRSV). They seem to recognize that any viable structure for human existence must involve God. But God is involved in their structure on *their* terms. They create the access to God and, by implication, they can remove it or alter it to suit their own needs whenever they want.

The crux of the story, however, is in the phrase "let us make a name for ourselves" (Gen 11:4 NRSV). Naming, biblically, relates to the identity of that which is named. The name is a manifestation of the essential nature of that which is named. Here we see decentered human existence, having lost the true center of human identity in loving union with God, attempting to determine for itself the nature of its own being.

You see then in the Cain and Babel stories the first biblical portrayals of the false self. Its essence is a mode of being in the world decentered from life in God, although seeking to retain God on its own terms; a mode of being that creates its own structures of identity, meaning, value and purpose; and a mode of being that determines for itself the nature of its own being.

SOME CONSEQUENCES OF BEING A FALSE SELF

When we identify our self as separate and apart from God—the essence of the false self—we also identify our self apart from everything else. We orient our self at a distance from others. We position ourselves "over against" the created order. Now that sounds like nice theology, perhaps, but we are beginning to realize in our day some of the horribly destructive consequences of this.

The history of human life on this planet is a long example of what happens when a person (or a community of persons) lives out of a posture of separateness with respect to others. This posture reduces others to objects to be manipulated for our purposes, whether those purposes be political, economic, social, cultural, religious, ethnic or whatever. When we meet resistance to our manipulation, we respond with violence of some sort that in turn results in a retaliatory violence by those on whom we inflicted our violence.

We are beginning to see in our world today the consequences of centuries of our self-referenced posture with respect to creation. The ecology of this planet is being destroyed because we have treated it as an object for us to manipulate and abuse as we desire in order to fulfill our self-referenced purposes.

The placing of our self in radical separation from God, others and creation—which is the essence of the false self—becomes a pervasive reality that poisons our life with God, with our self, with others and in the world.

You are probably wondering what this false self looks like. How does it manifest itself? What are its distinguishing characteristics? You may be particularly interested in how the false self might reveal itself in your life. Let's look at some of the basic attributes of the false self.

THE FALSE SELF IS A FEARFUL SELF

The false self is a fearful self. You find this reality early in the biblical story. After Adam and Eve usurped the place and role of God in their lives, after they became false selves, their first response to God's presence was "We were afraid" (Gen 3:10). In Romans 8, where Paul contrasts "life according to the flesh"—Paul's phrase for the false self—with "life according to the Spirit"—Paul's standard description of the true self—he writes, "For you did not receive a spirit of slavery to fall back into fear, but you have received a spirit of adoption. When we cry, 'Abba! Father!' it is that very Spirit bearing witness with our spirit that we are children of God" (Rom 8:15-16 NRSV).

Fear is the alternative to being a child of God, one whose spirit is in union with the Spirit of God. The roots of this fear go to the core of our false self. In the depths of our being, at a deep ontological level, our false self knows the roots of its identity are firmly planted in midair. There is no anchor for its being in something that is ultimately real. This loss of ultimate reality is sharply manifest in our postmodern culture, where the only ultimate reality is that there is no ultimate reality.

When we live as a false self we fear that our lack of a true center for our identity will be revealed and that weakness exploited by others. One of the ways our false self tries to compensate is to find our identity in performance. "I am what I do" is one of the primal perspectives of the false self. Our false self throws itself, often frantically, into a frenetic round of performances designed to provide a matrix of identity for our being. We engage in activities that affirm us as male or female, as heterosexual or homosexual or bisexual, as single or bonded to another, as husband or wife, as mother or father, as daughter or son, as employer or employee, as cultural or countercultural, as social or antisocial, as engaged with the world or disengaged from the world. The illustrations are endless. It is not that these activities are in themselves destructive of our true self. Many of them are the matrix within which our true self incarnates its reality in the created order. The problem is that in its primal fear our false self sinks the roots of our identity into these activities—activities that were never intended to bear the weight of our identity as children of God. God alone is capable of bearing the weight of our identity.

In addition, the only way we can know the true nature of our gender, sexuality and roles is by being in loving union with God at the core of our being. Once that loving union is broken, our understandings of gender, sexuality and roles are self-or culturally generated constructs designed to identify ourselves in contrast to all that is not us.

Let me illustrate this with another personal experience related to finding your identity in what you do. For seventeen years I was an upper-level administrator at the seminary where I teach. I never wanted this position. I did not seek it; it was thrust upon me. Throughout those years, whenever someone would ask me, "Do you enjoy your position?" I would reply, "*Enjoy* is not a term I relate to this role." I had convinced myself that none of the roots of my identity were entwined with this position. Then I resigned from that position and returned to full-time teaching. The first day I came on campus to go to my new office, my natural route took me by the office where I had spent the past seventeen years. With my mind on something else, I began instinctively to enter my old office. Then, suddenly, I became aware of how much the roots of my identity had become grounded in that office and its position. Here I had prided myself that this hadn't happened, but there it was, and it was a terrible wrenching within to turn my back on that office. The false self is so subtle in the ways it sinks its roots into things other than God, especially when you are engaged in God's work.

As our false self manages our life, we fear that we might not be valued. If our false self's identity is rooted in our performance, then our value must necessarily be rooted in how well we perform. Consequently, our false self attempts to perfect our performance, at least in our own estimation if not in the estimation of others. Our performance may be affirmed by the community or over against the community; it doesn't really matter which. All that matters is that our performance achieve that measure of success that provides our false self with the necessary affirmation of our value. How often a person is devastated when he or she is passed over for a promotion.

To the extent our false self guides our life, we fear others. Life with others is a constant threat to our false self. Others may see through or expose our façades of competence, confidence and control. Others may discover and disclose that we are a person without a firm center. Others may threaten our performance; they might even cause us to lose one or more of the performances by which we identify ourselves. They might outperform us and thereby demean our performance, calling into question our value. Others are constant threats to that fragile structure we have created to provide ourselves with identity, meaning, value and purpose. Others are also resistant if not downright opposed to our agenda for their place in our structure of life. How often do we refuse to move beyond our "comfort zone" because of this fear?

A secondary aspect of our false self's fear is anger. When we find ourselves unable to maintain a satisfactory matrix of identity, meaning, value and purpose in a world that constantly threatens to deconstruct that matrix, our false self is frequently angry at anyone or anything perceived to be thwarting our agenda. While such anger is usually directed at the perceived threat to our false self, it can also become a seething hostility that remains hidden beneath the surface of our false self, held in check by the need to maintain our false self's façade of control of our self and our world. When triggered by a sufficient threat, however, our anger boils to the surface in a rage often totally out of proportion to what triggered it. Have you ever had a person explode in your face at some very minor, insignificant thing?

Indeed, our false self is a fearful self. Isn't it interesting in the biblical story that when persons encounter the presence of God, often the first words spoken to them are "Do not be afraid."[4] Fear seems to be the inherent state of the false self.

THE FALSE SELF IS A PROTECTIVE SELF

A corollary of our false self's fear is our protectiveness. When we rely solely on our own resources for our identity, meaning, value and purpose, our false self, like Cain, constructs a "city" for itself. Our false self creates a complex matrix of perspectives and attitudes, habits of head and heart, patterns of behavior, structures of relationships, modes of relating and reacting to the surrounding world that not only serve to define our identity but also protect and defend us against real or imagined threats. We seek to amass for our self a treasure of resources with which we can strengthen our protective matrix. Our false self builds an extensive network of relationships, not merely to affirm our identity and value but as a resource that can be called on for defense in a time of threat to our identity and value. Our false self develops a treasury of material resources that again serve not only as an affirmation of our identity and value but also as a hedge against a loss of resources which would severely threaten our well-being. Since knowledge is power, our false self seeks to acquire an abundance of intellectual and informational resources. These enable our false self to extend its area of control and protect and defend us more vigorously.

Here is a possible illustration for you. How do you react while driving when another driver invades "your space," when they cut in front of you in traffic or pull out from a side road and force you to slow down or simply go slower than you had planned to go? Do you become aggressive, defending your space on the road, protecting your agenda for the trip? Isn't it amazing how our driving can manifest our false self?

You realize, I am sure, that networks of relationships, material resources, and intellectual and informational assets are not in themselves destructive. They are an integral part of human life, an essential aspect of human wholeness. It's when they become subverted to serve as the means to protect and preserve our false self that they become destructive.

THE FALSE SELF IS A POSSESSIVE SELF

You have probably seen the bumper sticker that reads, "The one who dies with the most toys wins!" The pathos of our false self is encapsulated here. Our false self sinks many of the tendrils of our identity and value into possessions. Jesus summarized the issue when he said, "For what will it profit them if they gain the whole world but forfeit their life?" (Mt 16:26 NRSV).

This essential nature of our false self is a primary factor in the modern economy of the West and, increasingly, in the economy of the world. Whenever something of our identity and value is grounded in our possessions, those possessions must always enhance our false self and its position in the world. Merely having enough is never sufficient when others have more. Having a standard brand is never enough when others have superior brands. Having the old model is never enough when the "new, improved" model is now available. The production industry's policy of planned obsolescence is based on our false self's need to always have the newer, better, improved product. The advertising industry is based largely on our false self's need to discover what we lack and our desire to have it. John Sharpe summarizes it well in his review of G.K. Chesterton's *Outline of Sanity:*

The world today operates by "...consuming the world's limited resources to produce an ever-expanding stream of products which are designed to wear out or become quickly outmoded, and for which the need is more often than not created by advertising, and not by necessity."[5]

Part of the possessive nature of our false self is interwoven with our fear and protectiveness. Possessions are seen as a means of protection against the threats that endanger our false self. Not only are possessions a hedge against the loss of material security, they can also be a valuable asset in manipulating the world in ways that protect our false self from threats to our status quo. A possible combination of these elements can be seen in the story of Ananias and Sapphira (Acts 5:1-11).

I think one of the most amazing consequences of the Pentecost experience of the gift of the Holy Spirit was the transformation of the believers from possessive persons to stewards. At the end of the account of Pentecost we are told: "All who believed were together and had all things in common; they would sell their possessions and goods and distribute the proceeds to all, as any had need" (Acts 2:44-45 NRSV). Doesn't it seem clear that the experience of the indwelling presence of God in their lives brought them to a new perspective toward their possessions? They came to realize that their possessions were resources entrusted to them by God and available to God for the welfare of others.

Ananias and Sapphira obviously did not share this perspective. But their false selves did not want to appear inferior to the rest of the community. Together they dreamed up a way they thought would give them the best of both worlds. They sold some property, as others had done (Acts 4:34-37), and by mutual agreement gave part of the proceeds to the community and retained the rest for themselves. In giving part of the proceeds to the community but letting the community think they were giving all the proceeds of the sale, Ananias and Sapphira were using their possessions to manipulate the community to look upon them favorably and to affirm their value and worth in the community. At the same time, by retaining a portion of the proceeds, they were maintaining a hedge against material insecurity. Ananias and Sapphira were motivated by the fear-driven protectiveness and possessiveness of the false self.

The reality of their false self is disclosed in the repeated reference to the state of their "heart." Peter asks, "Why has Satan filled your heart to lie to the Holy Spirit? ... How is it that you have contrived this deed in your heart?" (Acts 5:3-4 NRSV). It is clear that their heart was not centered in God. They were controlled by the possessiveness of the false self.

THE FALSE SELF IS A MANIPULATIVE SELF

Ananias and Sapphira also model for us one aspect of the manipulative nature of our false self. Our false self is a master manipulator, always seeking to leverage its world and all those in it in ways most advantageous to our own security, prestige and, especially, agenda. Having lost the true ground of our identity in loving union with God, where our real purpose in life is found, our false self must generate its own purpose.

If you or I were the only person in the world, this would not be a problem. However, we find ourselves surrounded by a community of false selves, all generating their own individual or corporate structures of purpose. Our false self finds itself enmeshed in a matrix of competing structures. Through subtle and not so subtle manipulations, we attempt to manipulate the matrix and those enmeshed in it to achieve our own purposes.

Here again our false self's deep-seated fear operates, always concerned that someone else might thwart its manipulations and diminish its purpose. When such possibilities begin to come true, our false self frequently reacts in anger toward the threat. From within this mode of being in the world emerge "enmities, strife, jealousy, anger, quarrels, dissensions, factions, envy" (Gal 5:20-21 NRSV).

At this point you need to realize that these characteristics of our false self are not merely individual aberrations.

The false self also has its collective manifestations: the neighborhood, the local community, the state, the nation, the clan, the tribe, the ethnic community, the church and religious institutions and systems. The characteristics of fearfulness, protectiveness, possessiveness and manipulation can all be seen in these corporate entities as well as in the individual.

Have you ever watched the TV drama *House?* Recently a series of episodes featured a wealthy person who gave one hundred million dollars to the hospital to make it a leading-edge research hospital. The "hook" in the gift was that the donor became the head of the hospital board. From this position he then began a program of blatant manipulation to reshape the hospital according to his agenda and purposes. It was a marvelous (terrible) illustration of both the possessiveness and manipulativeness of the false self.

THE FALSE SELF IS A DESTRUCTIVE SELF

When we operate as a false self we become destructive to ourselves, to others and to the world in which we live. Jesus said, "For those who want to save their life will lose it" (Mt 16:25 NRSV). To construct for ourselves an entire world of being alienated from God is to create a façade with no viable center. It is possible for our false self to gain an entire world for itself and lose its own soul. To be such a hollow person is to destroy our true self—a self created to find wholeness in a life of loving union with God that is, at the same time, a life in whom God's presence dwells for others. Not only does our false self contribute to the gradual deterioration of our deep inner life with God, it also contributes to mental, emotional and physical deterioration. The consequences of indulgences in smoking, overeating and unprotected sex can wreak a slow, insidious destruction in our physical existence. The indulgences of bitterness and resentment can result in a cancerous corrosion of our spirit.

As we seek to manipulate our world according to our own agenda, others become players in our false self's game. Others are valued largely for the benefit they can provide for us. When that value diminishes or disappears, they become expendable. Perhaps you have had the unfortunate experience of being warmly welcomed into a relationship, treated with attention and respect until you had fulfilled the purpose for which you were welcomed. Once you had fulfilled your expected role, you could sense the curtain of dismissal descend.

When we operate as a false self, the natural world becomes a commodity. Natural resources are used and abused to satiate our false self's compulsive need for more resources, more possessions, more control. At this point in human history we are beginning to see the global consequences of our false selves' rape of the planet to fulfill its own desires. We are destroying the very biosphere that sustains us and consuming nonrenewable resources at an ever increasing pace. When our insatiably increasing consumption of nonrenewable resources begins to drive up the cost of such consumption (such as oil), we are outraged that we have to pay more for our indulgences.

Our false self is like a virulent cancer destroying the other cells around it, destroying eventually the body and, along with it, itself.

THE FALSE SELF IS A SELF-PROMOTING SELF

When we take the place of God at the center of our life and world, our false self always promotes us and our agenda above all others. Even our most noble actions are undertaken with one eye on those who observe the actions and the other eye on the benefits the action will bring. The best of our behaviors become stained with the need for approval; the ultimate goal of the action is not the purpose integral to the action itself but the promotion of our value. Our false self may enter enthusiastically and vigorously into projects, join movements, serve on committees, run for office, but always our focus is on how such activities will enhance our prestige and solidify our identity.

A side effect of self-promotion is placing blame. Whenever our false self finds itself enmeshed in relationships or situations where something goes wrong, the immediate reaction is to fix blame in a manner that absolves us of most if not all culpability. Even when the cause for the problem lies clearly at the doorstep of our false self, we engage in rationalizations to mitigate our responsibility and excuse our failures. The recent debacle of the inhuman treatment of Iraqi prisoners at Abu Ghraib prison is a classic case study of the finger pointing, blame fixing, responsibility evading activity of the false self.

The common expression "What's in it for me?" discloses the heart of the self-promoting false self. There is a subtle dimension of our false self even though it is protective and defensive; on occasion our false self will undertake difficult and even dangerous actions knowing that such behavior provides esteem in the eyes of others. In a strange parody of Jesus' word, it even risks losing itself in order to gain itself on its own terms.

THE FALSE SELF IS AN INDULGENT SELF

Having lost our center in the One in whose presence is fullness of joy and at whose right hand are pleasures forevermore (Ps 16:11), our false self must find joy and pleasures elsewhere. Our now self-referenced desires must be fulfilled, not only to provide satisfaction and pleasure but to further authenticate our identity. Often our false self's primary purpose in life is the gratification of our desires.

Such gratification usually comes at the expense of others and of the world in which we live. Our false self gives little attention to the impact of the fulfillment of our desires on others and the world. Others are often simply the means for the fulfillment of our desires. At times, the fulfillment of our desires results in the diminishment of the quality or life or resources of others. Our false self's pandering to our wants results in economic imbalances that pull a large part of the world into deeper and deeper need. The West, with approximately 10 percent of the world's population, consumes far beyond 50 percent of the world's resources. In order to meet the ever growing demand of our false self for material pleasures, the environment is denuded and finite supplies of resources diminished.

Such gratification usually becomes a terrible compulsion, because nothing other than God can ultimately satisfy our hunger for joy and pleasure. Our false self exhausts the joy and pleasure of one endeavor only to move on to the next thing that promises to heighten our joy and deepen our pleasure. In some areas the compulsion becomes an addiction, and we find our self imprisoned in the destructive bondage of behaviors that have long since lost any semblance of joy and pleasure.

Our indulgent false self also keeps us at odds with others who may be competitors for the means of fulfilling our joy and pleasures. James epitomizes well the state of the indulgent false self and the nature of its conflicted relationships with others:

> Those conflicts and disputes among you, where do they come from? Do they not come from your cravings that are at war within you? You want something and do not have it; so you commit murder. And you covet something and cannot obtain it; so you engage in disputes and conflicts. You do not have, because you do not ask. You ask and do not receive, because you ask wrongly, in order to spend what you get on your pleasures. (Jas 4:1-3 NRSV)

Perhaps one of the most pathos-filled examples of the indulgence of our false self is seen in a TV advertisement that depicts a person at a carnival gorging himself on all manner of unhealthy food until he is bloated and sick with indigestion. Then the denouement of the solution—restraint, moderation, self-discipline? No way! The solution is the medication that will make the unpleasantness go away and clear the way for more indulgence. Our false self almost always treats symptoms rather than addressing the cause because to address the cause calls into question the viability of our false self.

THE FALSE SELF IS A DISTINCTION-MAKING SELF

Finally, our false self is characterized by a need to categorize others in ways that always give us the advantage. Since our false self is a way of being that positions us "over against" all others, others must be evaluated and labeled in such a way as to keep them either inferior to us or affirming and supportive "equals." We see a diverse array of such distinctions illustrated in the New Testament: Jew-Gentile, slave-free, male-female, circumcised-uncircumcised, barbarian-Scythian, rich-poor, wise-foolish, strong-weak. In all such instances, the one group identifies itself over against the other in a way that gives it superiority to the other. While most of the categories have changed in our day, the reality of such pejorative distinction-making is the same. This is but another means by which our false self attempts to secure our identity and enhance our value.

PAUL' S VERSION OF THE FALSE SELF

We have noted that the false self is what Paul describes when he writes about "life according to the flesh". Paul's "flesh life" is the pervasively self-referenced life of the false self. Paul provides us with a fairly pointed and painful description of the false self: "Now the works of the flesh are obvious: fornication, impurity, licentiousness, idolatry, sorcery, enmities, strife, jealousy, anger, quarrels, dissensions, factions, envy, drunkenness, carousing, and things like these" (Gal 5:19-21 NRSV).

You will notice that this is a list of activities that either protect, defend, promote, indulge or enable our false self to be in control of our life. Of course, all of the strife words (enmities, strife, jealousy, anger, quarrels, dissensions, factions, envy) represent two or more false selves interacting. For example, in my personal illustration at the beginning of this chapter, because my false self tried to control the lady at the X-ray machine in the airport, she immediately defended herself against my false self and off we went.

There is another place where Paul writes about this flesh life or false self. Paul says, "The inner orientation of the flesh[6] is hostile to God, it does not submit to God's law, indeed it cannot" (Rom 8:7). Paul is taking us back to the origins of the false self in Genesis 3. Our false self is a self that is playing god in our life. This raises what is for us the crucial problem of our false self. For Paul and for the rest of the biblical writers, the worst form of our false self is not some kind of blatant, rampant sensuality or gross material sins. For Paul the worst form of the false self is when it gets religion, when it becomes a religious false self. Paul is well equipped to instruct us on this because Paul has been there, done that. If you look at his testimony, Paul says, "If anyone thinks they have reason for confidence in the flesh [notice his use of the *flesh* term there], I have more"

(Phil 3:4). Paul is saying he can beat anyone in any argument about holiness: "Circumcised on the eighth day, of the people of Israel, of the tribe of Benjamin, a Hebrew of Hebrews, with respect to the law a Pharisee, with respect to zeal a persecutor of the church, with respect to righteousness under the law, blameless" (Phil 3:5-6). As far as Paul was concerned he had it all together. He was perfectly holy. What Paul discovered on the road to Damascus was that he was a religious false self—he was in control of his religiosity; he was in control of his relationship with God.

You can see why we must now look at the nature of the religious false self before we can consider the nature of our true self—a life of loving union with God and Christlike living in the world.

CONCLUSION

You have seen what happens when you pull the roots of your identity out of their true ground in God and sink them into something else as the source of your identity. You may sink those roots into your gender, and your maleness or your femaleness becomes the basic ground of who you are. You may sink those roots into your sexuality, and your sexual preferences become the ground of who you are. You may sink those roots into your ethnicity, and your ethnic identity becomes the basic ground of who you are. You may sink those roots into your culture, however you might define it for yourself, and your cultural identity becomes who you are. In our Western culture, you may sink your roots into what you do, and your functional identity becomes the ground of who you are. You may sink your roots into your possessions, and your economic identity becomes who you are.

As you probably realize, and as you think about your own false self, you don't sink your roots into just one thing other than God. You sink roots into all sorts of things, those we have listed and many others. The list could be expanded ad nauseam.

Our primary focus in this chapter, however, has been the defining characteristics of a self rooted in things other than God for its identity. These characteristics—fearful, protective, possessive, manipulative, destructive, self-promoting, indulgent, distinction-making—shape our perspectives, attitudes and behavior patterns.

The crucial problem is that these perspectives, attitudes and behavior patterns create a pervasive and deeply ingrained matrix of self-referenced being. This matrix develops so gradually over the years of our life—it is so subtly ingrained into us by our culture—that we are usually not even aware of its presence. We are like a fish that lives in water: unaware of the reality of water as the vital context of its life. Because our false self is so close to us, so much an integral part of who we are, we don't even realize it. This deeply entrenched matrix of self-referenced being is amazingly pervasive. Its stain colors all we are and all we do. Its perspective is the distorted lens through which we perceive ourselves and our world. It misshapes the nature of our thinking and communication. It taints all our relationships and makes the character of our reactions and responses to the world around us malignant.

None of the grounds we choose for rooting our identity are sufficient. None of them in and of themselves are necessarily bad, but they are not created to bear the weight of our being. When we seek to root our being in something other than God, we are a false self.

***

Gracious, loving God, O you of infinite patience and love and mercy and grace; awaken me in the depths of my being to those pervasive and corrosive dynamics of my false self, and especially those dynamics that have masked themselves behind a façade of religiosity, a semblance of spirituality; help me, gracious God, to let you meet me at the heart of this false self in ways that will enable me to abandon it to you and to let you, in love, draw the roots of my being into the very center of your being, that through the Holy Spirit you may nurture me into wholeness in your own image made

*known to me in Jesus, who with you
and the same Holy Spirit are worthy of
the full devotion of my life. Amen.*

3

THE IDOL IN THE BOX

The Religious False Self

Holy Mystery, you who are over all and through all and in all; you who are the source of my true being, help me as I read this chapter to be sensitive to what you may be saying to me in and through these thoughts and ideas. Help me, at any points of resistance, to let you meet me there and make that resistance a place of transforming grace. Help me, at those points where I too quickly agree, to let you open me up to the deeper dimensions of your truth that I may be avoiding by my easy assent. May this chapter become a place of transforming encounter with you, who together with Christ and the Holy Spirit are one God, the source

*of my true life now and forever.
Amen.*

A friend of mine once said, as he began the second of a two-lecture series, "The first step is the hardest. Then it gets more difficult!" The same could be said in dealing with our false self. The reality of this pervasive, deeply entrenched, self-referenced structure of being as the primary context of our spiritual journey is one of the hardest things for us to acknowledge. We tend to think of it as a "surface phenomena" that can be treated by a few cosmetic alterations in our behavior. We are slow to accept the fact that our false self is who we are all the way to the core of our being. We are profoundly habituated to a self-referenced way of being in the world. Jesus makes this unmistakably clear when he says, "If anyone would come after me, they must deny themselves," and, "Whoever loses their self for my sake will find it" (Mt 16:24-25). Jesus is not talking about giving up candy for Lent. He is calling for the abandonment of our entire, pervasive, deeply entrenched matrix of self-referenced being.

It is even more difficult, however, for us to acknowledge the reality of our religious false self. Our religious false self presumes, because we are religious, that everything is fine in our relationship with God. Oh, to be sure, there may be a need for some "fine-tuning" of a few aspects of our life, a polishing up of a few of our rough edges. Our religious false self may be rigorous in religiosity, devoted in discipleship and sacrificial in service—without being in loving union with God.

We see a frightening example of this at the end of the Sermon on the Mount. Jesus depicts a scene before the throne on the judgment day. A group of people appear there and say, "Lord, Lord, did we not prophesy in your name, and cast out demons in your name, and do many deeds of power in your name?" Obviously these were serious, dedicated disciples. Their lives had been spent doing "God things." But Jesus replies to them, "I never knew you; go away from me, you evildoers" (Mt 7:22-23 NRSV). Their lives, their ministries, were not grounded in a loving union with Christ.

They were religious false selves. They were so busy *being in the world for God* that they failed to *be in God for the world.* There is a great difference between these two ways. A religious false self will expend amazing amounts of energy and resources to be in the world for God. But you see, we are called to be in God for the world, and this is costly. It requires the abandonment of the whole self-referenced structure of our false self and, especially, the religious false self. Oswald Chambers says it well: "Salvation is not merely deliverance from sin, nor the experience of personal holiness; the salvation of God is deliverance out of self entirely into union with Himself."[1]

Perhaps the premier examples of religious false selves in the New Testament are the Pharisees. Jesus uses a powerful simile to describe their frightening condition. He calls them "whitewashed tombs" that outwardly appear beautiful but within are full of deadness (Mt 23:27). Their outward display of religiosity was enviable in its apparent holiness, in its faithful obedience to the Torah, in its devotion to the scribal lists of dos and don'ts, in its rigorous abstention from anything that might defile its purity. Behind this religious façade, however, was an emptiness of deadly proportions. Their profound religiosity was a self-generated effort at attaining holiness for themselves rather than the fruit of a life in loving union with God.

For those of us on an intentional spiritual journey, our awareness of the deadly and debilitating nature of the religious false self is essential. Rigorous religious practices, devoted discipleship, sacrificial service, deeper devotional activities may do nothing more than turn a nominally religious false self into a fanatically religious false self.

THE NATURE OF THE RELIGIOUS FALSE SELF

The essential characteristics of the religious false self are exactly the same as those of the false self we looked at in the previous chapter. Rather than revisit our list, let's look at some of the ways the wolfish characteristics of our false self clothe themselves in the sheep's clothing of religiosity.

The essential difference between a false self and a religious false self is that the latter brings God into its life. Our religious false self may begin with a genuine experience with God. But then, like Peter on the mount of transfiguration (Mt 17:1-4), we often seek to contain our experience within a box of our own making. We attempt to integrate our experience with God into the structures of our life in ways that are minimally disruptive to our status quo. The "God"[2] within our box, however, becomes a construct, an idol, that enables us to maintain control of what we call "God" as well as continue to be in control of our existence. To put it succinctly, whenever we attempt to have God in our life on our terms, we are a religious false self.

Fear. To be sure, we construct for ourselves a core that we call "God," but this is not the living Reality who is the true matrix of our identity. When this is the nature of our relationship with God, there is an inherent fear that this "God" may not be adequate in all our relationships and circumstances, that this "God" may not perform as we desire. So we continually tinker with the idol we call "God" in futile efforts to upgrade the idol and make it more suitable for us and more under our control. Some of us do this by education, learning more about God, believing that if only we can get our minds around God and understand God better we will be better able to have God in our life on our terms. Others of us do this by shopping from church to church attempting to find a "God" that is suitable for us. We also regularly refurbish the box of doctrine and practices in which we keep our idol to protect it against threats that might call its viability into question. All these, of course, are exercises in futility. Any God we have in our life on our terms is an idol.

A greater fear of our religious false self is that the idol we call "God" may be revealed as false. We fear that the box may be empty! This fear is well grounded. The constructs we call "God" *are* false; the boxes of dogma, theology, liturgy and doctrine within which we attempt to contain and control God *are* empty.

Our religious false self will spend inordinate amounts of energy refining our idol and embellishing its box with layers of theology, doctrine and liturgy. This may be a manifestation of the greatest fear of our religious false self—that the true and living God might become manifest and shatter the idol and blow the walls out of the box.

Thomas Carlson frames the issue well in his synopsis of Jean-Luc Marion's critique of modern theological constructs of "God":

> "God" ... amounts to a "conceptual" idol in which some well-defined and therefore limited concept of "God," some predication of God's essence made present to the mind, is taken to be equivalent with God himself; such a concept and predication, ... really constitute only an invisible mirror of purely human thought.[3]

In a very real sense the crux of our journey from our religious false self to our true self is an ever deepening abandonment of the construct we call

"God" and an ever more profound willingness for God to be whatever God will be in our life at any given moment.

Our religious false self has another fear: that others might discover its religiosity is a façade. This fear may manifest itself in at least three ways. We may become very individual and privatized in our religiosity. By isolating our self from others we insulate our self from the threat they and their idols represent to our idol. Our isolation can be physical or, in most cases, theological. We simply marginalize everyone whose idol is a threat to ours, thus preserving the security of our idol. This leads to the second way our fear of others manifests itself. We may seek a community of faith whose idol is very much the same as ours and whose box has much of the same character and adornment as ours. By this means, our religious false self not only protects our frail idol in its fragile box but finds support and encouragement in a community of "faith" for maintaining that idol in that box. The third way in which our religious false self deals with its fear is to adopt the pluralistic perspective of our postmodern age, which allows us to maintain the validity of our idol in its box without being intolerant of others and the idols in their boxes.

Often our religious false self hides its fear behind a wall of activity. Our religious false selves can be as frenetic in our religiosity as secular false selves are in their performance-oriented attempts to authenticate their identity and value. A welter of worship services, Bible studies, prayer meetings, accountability groups, fellowship meetings, retreats and workshops often enable us to calm our fears and assure ourselves that our religious identity and value is secure. Of course, the praise and adulation we usually receive for all these activities further serve to confirm the validity of our idol and the box in which it is kept.

A secondary aspect of our religious false self's fear is anger. The secular world that regularly devalues religion, other religions that provide competition and other religious false selves constantly threaten to decenter our religious false self's idol and denigrate its box. Thus our religious false self is often an angry self. We are angry at anyone or anything perceived to be threatening our "God" and the structures of perception and ritual in which our "God" is contained and controlled. Such anger can, especially in our religious false self, become a seething hostility that remains hidden beneath the surface, held in check by the need to maintain the façade of religiosity. When triggered by a sufficient threat, however, our anger boils to the surface in a rage often totally out of proportion to what triggered it, and we often excuse it as righteous indignation.

I suspect that as you have been reading this section, you have thought of persons who in some sense have illustrated for you the fearful behaviors of a religious false self. Perhaps you may even have caught a glimpse of yourself peeking out from the text. If so, then let these points become touches of grace awakening you to the need to abandon the idol you call "God," and calling you into a deeper relationship of loving union with the living God.

Protection. Whenever our identity is rooted in an idol we call "God," we become very protective of that "God." Our religious false self constructs strong fortifications of theology, doctrine, dogma and liturgy to contain and protect our "God." We develop lists of dos and don'ts that define for us the practices of life which are expected of anyone who believes in our "God."

When anyone even suggests an alternative theology, a different doctrine, an opposing dogma, a variant liturgy, our religious false self rises up to defend the truth against these "heresies." The bitter battles that have characterized Christian history—schisms, denominational splits, and church divisions—bear sad testimony to this defensive aspect of our religious false self. Inquisitions have come in many guises, but behind them all is a religious false self seeking to protect the "God" it has constructed for itself.

Some of us, as religious false selves, often seek a church where the people by and large have the same "God" we do. While there may be some space for slight variations in the nature of this

"God," any major deviations are not tolerated, and those with the temerity to suggest such variations are quickly brought into line or made to feel unwanted. The walls of defense can be harsh and cold.

Others of us don't appear at first blush to be so protective of our "God." In a spirit of pluralism and toleration, we are willing to allow almost any "God," so long as others allow us to have our "God." These religious false selves, however, become extremely intolerant of anyone who even suggests that there may be only one ultimate reality. Their tolerant pluralism is never broad enough to include those whom they see as intolerant nonpluralists. So, in their protectiveness, they too become intolerant and narrow pluralists.

Like Cain, our religious false selves construct a city for ourselves and believe it is the "city of God." Our complex matrix of religious perspectives and attitudes, habits of head and heart, patterns of behavior, structures of relationships, modes of relating and reacting to the surrounding world serve to define our religious identity. Our religious false self seeks to amass a treasure of theological, ecclesiological and religious resources with which we can strengthen our protective matrix. We may build an extensive network of religious relationships, not merely to affirm the identity and value of our "God" but as a resource that can be called on for defense in a time of threat to our identity and value.

There are even some religious false selves who surround themselves with a treasury of material resources that are viewed both as God's blessing and as an affirmation and defense of the correctness of their "God."

Since knowledge is power, religious false selves often seek to acquire control of religious intellectual and informational resources such as colleges, seminaries and publishing houses. While sound doctrine and the affirmation of denominational distinctives are important, these must never become idolatrous. Doctrines and distinctives become idolatrous when they are used to protect and defend an idol called "God."

You certainly know that networks of relationships, material resources, and intellectual and informational assets are not in themselves destructive. They are an integral part of human life, an essential aspect of human wholeness. They become destructive whenever they become subverted to serve as the means to protect and preserve the "God" of our religious false self.

Possessiveness. One aspect of the possessiveness of our religious false self is seen in another dimension of the story of Ananias and Sapphira we looked at in chapter two. This couple was active in the new community of believers in Jesus, where the sharing of possessions within the community for the welfare of all was the norm. As typical religious false selves, Ananias and Sapphira did not want to appear to be acting contrary to the community. If they did, it might appear that their "God" was different from that of the community. So in order to appear to be following the community ethos, they too sold a piece of property but connived together to hold some of the proceeds for themselves. They made a presentation to the community that purported to be the full amount. As we know, their plan failed horribly. The real crux of the issue, however, was not simply their possessiveness for material security. The problem was their possessiveness of their religiosity. They wanted to possess their religious status in the eyes of the community, to appear as full participants in the religious life of the community.

When the idol we call "God" becomes a significant part of our identity, we become very possessive of our "God." The same is true when a community's identity becomes defined by its "God." The possessive pronouns begin to dominate the community's vocabulary: my/our church, my/our theology, my/our creed, my/our denomination, my/our worship style. There are those whose protective possessiveness is so great that they take control of the church or denomination to insure that the "God" who forms their religious identity is assured of proper maintenance and security.

Manipulation. Our religious false self is a master manipulator, always seeking to leverage our religious world and all those in it in ways most advantageous to its security, its prestige and, especially, our religious agenda.

Perhaps, in a community of faith you know or have been part of, there were those whose "God" was not quite fully and faithfully represented by the larger community. If they were religious false selves, they may have worked their way into positions of power so they could manipulate the larger community to make their "God" normative for the community. In denominations there are likewise those who seek positions of power in order to steer an entire denomination into the adoption of their "God." In both instances, when such religious false selves get into power, they put in place structures, policies and procedures that effectively restrict any opposing perspective from being seriously considered. Here we see one of the most detrimental aspects of the manipulation of religious false selves.

But it gets worse! Our religious false self is also characterized by a manipulative relationship with the idol we call "God." Much if not all of our religiosity is an attempt to manipulate "God" to love us, care for us and fulfill our desires and needs according to our agendas. Our prayer, rather than an abandonment of ourselves to God for God's purposes in and through us, is an enlistment of God to endorse our purposes. Rather than wanting God in our life on God's terms, our religious false selves want God in our lives on our terms.

Perhaps the most insidious aspect of the manipulative nature of our religious false self is that its manipulation is done in the name of God. Rarely if ever do we admit to others or to our self that our manipulations are for our own purposes. Our purposes and agendas have become "God's" purposes, "God's" agenda, and we are simply agents of "God."

You might give some thought to how much of our evangelism is manipulative. Rather than awakening persons to the presence of God in their lives, rather than leading them into a transforming relationship with Christ, we manipulate them into thinking as we think, believing as we believe, worshiping as we worship, and coming to church dressed as we are and behaving as we do. We make them clones of ourselves, people who have the same idol called "God" as we do.

Destructive. You undoubtedly realize that such cloning is destructive. Persons are cloned into religious false selves rather than nurtured into loving union with God and being Christlike in the world. Perhaps the greatest destructiveness of our religious false self is our delusion that we really have a relationship with God and that everything is perfectly in order as far as God is concerned. Here again Paul is a prime example. In his testimony as a holy Pharisee (Phil 3:4-6), Paul sums up his entire relationship with God in the words "As to righteousness under the Law, blameless!" (v. 6). Paul, the epitome of a religious false self, believed that he was in absolutely perfect relationship with God. So sure was Paul, he saw himself as being responsible for bringing to judgment those whose "God" did not conform to his. Paul was completely confident that he was in the center of God's will in his persecution of the Christians. After all, believing in a crucified carpenter as the Messiah was not only "out of the box" but beyond any rational consideration at all. It was a perversion of everything associated with Paul's "God."

Listen to Paul's reflections on his religious false self:

> These very things that were gain for me I have come to consider as loss on account of Christ. But more than that, I have come to consider everything to be loss on account of the greater value of the knowledge of Christ Jesus my Lord, on account of whom I have suffered the loss of all things and consider them as dung in order that I might gain Christ and be found in him, not having a right relationship with God based on my keeping the Law, but the right relationship with God which is through the faith of Christ, the right relationship of God based on that faith. (Phil 3:7-9)

Paul's expression of the loss of his religious false self is epitomized in the term *dung,* translating a Greek word meaning "dog's droppings."[4] For Paul, his religious false self was worth no more than a pile of dog dung. The "right relationship with God [righteousness] based on my keeping the Law" expresses the self-referenced focus and self-generated religiosity of Paul's religious false self. Paul's testimony is a vivid portrayal of the self-destructiveness of the religious false self. Paul thought he was in a perfect relationship with God only to discover how wrong he was.

Our religious false self can be a destructive cancer in a community of faith. We can spread the poison of judgmentalism against those whose "God" is different. We can pour the corrosive acid of criticism and bitterness into situations that are not compatible with our perspective. We can engender a disruptive spirit of factionalism and divisiveness, demonizing opponents and crucifying those who oppose us. Where our religious false self is not so overt in its destructive presence, it is often a malignant growth of resentment, unforgiveness and meanness of spirit beneath the surface of the community's life.

We can see the destructiveness of a communal religious false self in churches that become ingrown cliques or religious social clubs for the pious elite, carefully delimiting themselves from outsiders lest anyone or anything disturb their comfortable status quo. Such communities of religious false selves rarely exhibit compassion for the world at their door. The prophetic vision of being God's people in the world is dead, and the idea of abandonment to God in love and availability to God for others never crosses their mind.

In an even more serious vein the religious false self, in both its individual and corporate forms, is destructive to the image of the faith and the church in the nonbelieving world. The world, observing the activities of the religious false self, whether in individual or corporate form, sees nothing that speaks to its own woundedness, bondage and despair. It sees only its own sin, darkness and death mirrored back through an unpalatable religious veneer.

Self-promotion. Jesus warns his followers against the self-promotion of the religious false self:

> *Beware of practicing your piety before others in order to be seen by them;* for then you have no reward from your Father in heaven.
>
> So whenever you give alms, do not sound a trumpet before you, as the hypocrites do in the synagogues and in the streets, *so that they may be praised by others.* Truly I tell you, they have received their reward....
>
> And whenever you pray, do not be like the hypocrites; for they love to stand and pray in the synagogues and at the street corners, *so that they may be seen by others.* Truly I tell you, they have received their reward. (Mt 6:1-2, 5 NRSV, emphasis added)

Our religious false self is, by and large, a carefully crafted façade. Paul writes to Timothy of those who have the "outward form of godliness but deny its power" (2 Tim 3:5). Our religious false self seeks to create a life that appears to others, to us and, we hope, to God as a life of deep religiosity.

In some of us the façade is merely a genteel form of religious social propriety, a concomitant part of a proper presence in the community. For others the façade is an "in your face" religiosity that takes seeming delight in flaunting itself against the prevailing ethos and mores of the larger community. For some of us the façade is only maintained when we are participating in the religious community and is handily modified or even discarded in the everyday world. For others the façade is maintained in any and all circumstances, often in inappropriate ways, because the façade itself is an essential part of our identity as a religious false self.

Indulgence. There are at least two ways in which our religious false self is indulgent—in its religiosity and in its nonreligiosity.

Since our religious false self finds our identity in the idol we call "God," we frequently indulge our self in an excess of religious practices that affirm our idol. Such indulgence can take two opposite forms. One form is a rigid retention of the liturgies and practices that have come to define our idol. A particular worship style itself becomes idolized and anything that threatens that style is anathema. This aspect of our religious false self is seen on both sides of the worship wars rending religious communities across denominations. The other form of indulgence is an incessant quest for ever new and more fulfilling forms of liturgy and practice to adorn the idol.

Another form of religious indulgence often practiced by our religious false self is the amassing of religious practices that become a matter of religious pride. Attendance records in worship, Sunday school, Bible study or prayer meetings; unfailing daily practice of Bible reading and prayer; service on boards and committees of the church; all, when motivated by pride, are indulgences of our religious false self.

There is, however, a very different kind of indulgence practiced by our religious false self. Often our religious false self will be characterized by indulgence in behaviors that are clearly contrary to Christlikeness and even contrary to the standards of our religious false self itself. Our religious false self may justify such behavior as a reward for being so religious in other areas. We may claim that this indulgence is earned because so much has been sacrificed to be religious.

This kind of indulgence reveals the hollow and unsubstantial nature of our religious false self. The façade of religiosity is insufficient to deal with the deep brokenness and bondage, woundedness and sin, deadness and darkness that scar the human soul. The façade only covers over the problem; it doesn't cleanse and heal, liberate and transform.

Finally, our religious false self is characterized by our need to categorize others in ways that always give us the advantage.

Distinctions. This distinction-making aspect is seen in the terrible gulfs that often divide denominations and groups within denominations. It is found in the theological wars that rage between those of various theological persuasions.

It is destructively manifested in the ways in which religious false selves categorize themselves and demonize those at the opposite end of the chosen spectrum of categorization: l i b e r a l - c o n s e r v a t i v e , e v a n g e l i c a l - e c u m e n i c a l , C a l v i n i s t - A r m i n i a n , h o m o p h i l e - h o m o p h o b e , feminist-chauvinist.

This is by no means to say that genuine faith is some sort of homogeneous, uniform, identical and unvarying set of beliefs and practices. Nor is it to say that there are no genuine theological differences, that wisdom and discernment are unnecessary. What our religious false self does, however, is to fasten on our position along the trajectory of belief and practice as the only reality, and identify our self by its distinction over and against all others on that trajectory. This makes our religious false self's identity dependent not on union with God in love but on our difference from the other.

PAUL THE EXPERT

Paul is an expert in the religious false self. He knows the reality from deep within its structure. He can speak to us with authority about its terrible dangers and deadly consequences.

One of the places Paul unpacks these dangers and consequences most pointedly is in Colossians 2:20-23. This is the first unit of a very carefully crafted, compact and complete portrayal of the Christian life (Col 2:20—3:17) that moves us from our religious false self toward a deeper life in loving union with God in Christ. We can see the basic flow of the passage by looking at the theme portions of the units:

2:20-23: "Since you died with Christ..."

3:1-4: "Since you were raised with Christ..."

3:5-11: "Put to death therefore..."

3:12-17: "Put on therefore..."

There is a very tightly woven pattern here: two contrasts—

1. "Since you died..."   Since you were raised..."

2. "Put to death..."   "Put on..."

and two parallelisms—

1. "Since you died..."   "Put to death..."

2. "Since you were   "Put on..."
raised..."

In the next chapters we will work our way through this entire passage to plumb the depths of Paul's understanding of the Christian life as one of growing union with God in love and incarnate in lives available to God for others.

In 2:20-23, however, Paul's focus is the same as our present chapter, our religious false self. Paul begins his description of the Christian life by a strong warning against the religious false self. He introduces the issue by stating, "Since your death with Christ liberated you from the controlling powers of your world, then why is your life still under their domination?"[5] Several points require explanation here.

Since your death with Christ. Paul realizes that in the death of Christ the totality of our false self was confirmed as dead. He makes this explicit in 2 Corinthians 5:14-15: "We are convinced that one [Christ] has died for all;

therefore *all have died"* (v. 14 NRSV, emphasis added). The significance of this becomes clear when Paul continues, "And he died for all in order that those who live might live no longer for themselves [the epitome of the self-referenced life of our false self], but for him [a Christ-referenced life] who died and was raised for them" (v. 15). Paul is not simply theologizing here; he is speaking of spiritual realities at the deepest levels. In the death of Christ something related to the very essence of our false self took place—its deadness was irrevocably confirmed. Thus, for Paul, when persons enter into a loving relationship with Christ they enter first into his death. He asks the Romans, "Do you not know that all of us who have been baptized into Christ Jesus were baptized into his death?" (Rom 6:3 NRSV). Two verses later Paul indicates that union with Christ begins in being "united with him in a death like his," and to Timothy he writes, "If we have died with him, we will also live with him" (2 Tim 2:11 NRSV, cf. Rom 6:8). It is this reality Paul states succinctly in Colossians 3:3: "You have died!"

What does this mean for us? Such a death is both a deep inner acknowledgment of our false self and a radical commitment to abandon our self-referenced mode of being. This is why we will see Paul exhort us later to "put to death the controlling dynamics of the false self" (Col 3:5).[6] Our dying with Christ is, ultimately, the loss of everything that has defined us. It is our utter rejection of all that has falsely determined our identity, value, meaning and purpose. It is losing the entirety of our false self for Christ's sake (Mt 10:39).

Liberated you from the controlling powers of your world. This is why Paul qualifies our death with Christ as having "liberated you from the controlling powers of your world." The Greek for "the controlling powers of your world" points to those spiritual forces and powers that were believed to control human life in the world of Paul's day. The analogue in our day is the individual and communal structures of the self-referenced being of our false self, the norms by which society in general and, more specifically, subgroups within the culture expect us to live, the values and perspectives that shape our individual and collective life in the world. Paul's claim is radical. Participation in the death of Christ liberates us from the entire matrix of self-referenced dynamics that have misshaped our life and our culture.

The radical nature of this liberation is illustrated by the burning of the books of magic in Ephesus (Acts 19:19). Magic in the first-century world was the means by which a person could gain some measure of control over the "controlling powers of the world." Book burning in those days was usually undertaken by those in power in order to repudiate and eradicate dangerous movements. In Ephesus we see the owners of the books burning them themselves, a public witness of their repudiation of all that magic represented as well as a witness to the liberation they had found through Christ. Another evidence to the radical nature of Christ's liberation is the value of the books—50,000 silver coins, the equivalent of about 140 years' wages for a day laborer. Paul, then, is pointing us to a profound and radical restructuring of our life when, in Christ, we accept the deadness of our false self and repudiate its whole structure of being. We are then liberated from its destructive and dehumanizing bondage.

Here is a contemporary illustration. When I was in pastoral ministry I became friends with an atheist with whom I had long discussions about philosophy, the meaning of life and, eventually, at his leading, the Christian life and belief. After long months of friendship and conversation, he called to make an appointment to see me at my office in the church (all our other conversations had been in his home). When he arrived he sat down and pulled a slip of paper from his shirt pocket and held it in his hands. He then asked me, "What do I have to do to become a Christian?" I explained to him that he need only respond to God's love for him in Christ by thankfully receiving that love and offering himself to Christ in love.

He then lifted up his slip of paper and asked, "What about all this stuff?" He had listed there the controlling powers that shaped the matrix of his self-referenced life—alcohol, pornography, nicotine and so forth. I explained to him that you didn't become a Christian by giving up things (he would have simply become a religious false self) but by giving your life to Christ and loving him more than these things. I assured him that if he did this, that Christ would take care of all this stuff.

Several weeks later he responded to an altar call during the worship service and gave himself to Christ. In fairly short order, his growing relationship with Christ resulted in his liberation from the controlling powers that had previously misshaped his life.

Then why is your life still under their domination? Now Paul puts his finger on the focal issue of our religious false self. He is obviously writing to people who have made some kind of commitment to Christ. They have professed faith and been baptized into his death (Col 2:10-14). Yet their lives appear to be still under the domination of those controlling powers that ordered their lives before they became Christians. Here Paul surprises us. We would expect him to give a list of behaviors that epitomize a life dominated by the controlling powers of the world or perhaps a list of vices such as we will find in Colossians 3:5, 8. Instead, Paul illustrates the problem by saying, "Why are you living by rules like, 'Do not handle. Do not taste. Do not touch?'" These do not appear to describe profligate, sensual, corrupt behaviors. This is not a list of vices. It is rather a list of activities that suggests scrupulous religiosity. These people appear to be doing everything in their power to live lives of perfect holiness, abstaining from even touching anything that might defile their religiosity.

Doesn't this sound sadly familiar? How often do we find persons and churches who define the Christian life by abstinence from certain practices and behaviors. *Detachment* from these practices and behaviors becomes the primary focus of their life rather than an ever deepening *attachment* to God in love. If detachment is not the consequence of loving attachment to God, then our religiosity is shaped by our detachment, and we have become religious false selves.

All these things result in perishing with use. Then Paul gives us the first blow of a one-two punch against our religious false self: "All these things result in perishing with use."[7] What is used if nothing is handled, tasted or touched? Nothing! Then what perishes? Paul is indicating that it is the user who will perish by trying to be holy through the means of such practices. Such self-generated lists of dos and don'ts, and such self-referenced efforts to be holy, are doomed to failure because, as Paul indicates, "they are merely human rules and teachings." They are human-centered and human-generated attempts to be religious. They are activities of our religious false self.

Paul next points to one of the most dangerous aspects of our religious false self: "These activities have an appearance of wisdom in rigorous religiosity, seeming humility, even severe asceticism" (Col 2:23). The façade of our religious false self can be very convincing. We appear to be extremely committed, deeply pious, thoroughly religious. This statement is Paul's version of Jesus' depiction of the Pharisees, whose holiness was like whitewashed tombs; they appeared beautiful to the outside observer but inside there was nothing but deadness and uncleanness (Mt 23:27).

But they are of no value at all, they only satisfy the flesh. Now Paul gives the second and knockout punch to our religious false self: "but they are of no value at all, they only satisfy the flesh." For Paul there are only two modes of human existence: life according to the flesh and life according to the Spirit (Rom 8). Paul's "life according to the flesh" is what we have described as the false self. It is, as Paul says, living for ourselves (2 Cor 5:15), a pervasive structure of self-referenced being. The worst form of the flesh life in Paul's eyes is when it becomes religious. The religious false self is anathema for Paul. Having been the epitome of a religious false self, Paul knows deep within his being the terrible danger it poses. The fraudulent façade of our religious false self deceives others and deludes us.

Thus Paul begins his portrayal of the Christian life as a growth in loving union with God by setting forth the strongest possible warning against the terrible danger of our religious false self—a self who wants a relationship with God on our terms. Our religious false self wants to keep our "God" in the box of our control.

At this point you may need to probe your motives for reading this book.

- Are you on a genuine quest for radical abandonment to God in love, or are you simply seeking a stronger form of the religious false self?

- I am sure you want God in your life; you probably would not be reading this book unless you did. But do you want God in your life on your terms, or on God's?

- How much of your present spirituality is the manifestation of a religious false self?

- Is your journey one of abandonment to God or one of acquisition from God? That is, is your journey energized by the desire to get something for yourself spiritually or is your journey energized by the desire to abandon yourself to God?

Before we move forward into the next chapters to the alternative to our religious false self—our true self, a life of radical abandonment to God in love—we must be clear on the nature of our religious false self and must come to the decision to lose this life for Christ's sake.

4

HIDDEN WITH CHRIST IN GOD

The False Self and the Christ Self

> *Gracious and merciful God, whose <u>cruciform</u> love has plumbed the depths of my false self, awaken me from the pervasive bondage of my false self and enable me through the power of your indwelling Holy Spirit to be restored to wholeness in the image of Christ. As I look into the nature of this Christ self, stir my heart to hunger and thirst for your transforming work in my life through the Holy Spirit, who with Christ lives and reigns with you. Amen.*

We have now made our way through the jungle of our false self and its religious manifestations and have arrived at the border where our false self and our true self meet. We will now consider who we were created to be, the horrible position our false self has put us in, God's profound solution to our irresolvable dilemma, and how we deny our false self and begin to be a true self hidden with Christ in God.

WHO WE ARE

The revelation of our true nature comes quite early in the biblical story when God says, "Let us make humanity in our own image," and in the next verse, "God created humanity in God's own image, male and female God created them" (Gen 1:26-27). This is the first indication of a profound reality that threads its way through all the rest of the biblical story. We are persons created in the image of God.

Paul, however, gives us a radically profound insight into the reality of who we are that frames our identity in a whole new paradigm. Paul writes in Ephesians, "Blessed be the God and Father of our Lord Jesus Christ, who has blessed us in Christ with every spiritual blessing in the heavenly places" (Eph 1:3 NRSV). Now this alone transforms our self perspective. Do you habitually, regularly think of your life as being immersed in blessing? Just as a fish lives its life immersed in water, our lives are immersed in blessing.

If you are like me, you would probably answer, "Not all the time." You know there are those times when it certainly doesn't seem as though your life is immersed in blessing. I remember such a time a few years ago. I was recovering from hernia surgery and was taking my first trip to attend a committee meeting in Nashville. While I was there, word came that my mother-in-law had just died. We had been a three-generation family for twenty-six years. My wife and her mother were having a theological discussion at breakfast. Right in the middle of the discussion, her mother simply left. The same day, my daughter and I were served papers that we were being sued for an automobile accident that my daughter had a few months earlier. About a week later, I went for my regular check-up with my dermatologist. I had already had one skin cancer surgery, and there was this little lump on the back of my neck that concerned me. The dermatologist looked at it and did a biopsy, and sure enough, it was another basal cell carcinoma. So just as I recovered from one surgery, I had to have another surgery. Now it certainly didn't seem like my life was immersed in blessing those couple of months, but Paul is saying our life *is* immersed in blessing.

As I wrestled with this, I began to get a glimmer of understanding of some of those impossible commands that Paul gives us. For instance, "Rejoice always" (Phil 4:4).

I don't know about you, but I want to say to Paul, "Hey, Paul, how about rejoice some of the time? I can handle that, but this 'rejoice always' stuff? Come on, Paul. Get real."

Paul responds, "In nothing be anxious" (Phil 4:6).

Sure! Right! Paul, you don't know the stressors in my life. You don't know the problems I'm facing. You don't know my difficulties. In nothing be anxious? In what kind of ivory tower do you live your life?

Paul comes right back and says, "In everything give thanks" (v. 6).

I am about ready to give up on this guy. Sure, I can give thanks for some things. Perhaps I might even be able to give thanks most of the time. But in *everything* give thanks? Paul sounds like a seminary professor sitting in his ivory tower spinning out these wonderful theological theories! What he asks is totally unrealistic.

When Paul wrote these injunctions, however, he was sitting in a Roman dungeon not sure that he would get out with his life. Now, to be sure, he's pretty sure he will be released (Phil 1:19, 25-26), but then, in Philippians 2:17, he says, "Even if I am to be poured out as a sacrificial offering on the altar of your faith I rejoice." He does what? He *rejoices.* Paul either has slipped over the edge of sanity or else has discovered a reality that we need to discover.

I believe what Paul had discovered was that his life was immersed in blessing. That is why he could say to the Romans, "In everything God works for good" (Rom 8:28).

Oh, come on, Paul. Let me tell you some of my "everythings."

Paul discovered that there is another order of being, there is another structure of life in which life, even life in a Roman dungeon, is immersed in blessing.

At this point, I say to myself, *Well now, that's probably true for Paul.* After all, Paul is a rather important person in God's scheme of things. He is the great apostle to the Gentiles. He wrote most of the New Testament. Paul is very significant; it makes sense that his life is immersed in blessing. But who am I? I believe this is why Paul continues as he does in Ephesians 1:4: our lives are immersed in blessing "just as God chose us before the foundation of the world, that we should be holy and blameless before God in love."

Chose is the operative word here. It represents a compound Greek word formed with a preposition meaning "forth from" or "out of" and the verb "to speak." Its woodenly literal meaning is "to speak forth." If you were to call on a member of a group to come forward and assist you in some activity, you would be speaking them forth from the rest of your options. You would be choosing them. So the translation "chose" is fine, but it doesn't carry the thrust of what Paul is saying. When you put "spoke forth" together with the next phrase, "before the foundation of the world," where do you think Paul's Hebrew brain is? Paul is back in Genesis 1, where God "spoke forth" creation into being. In fact, Paul has gone back to Genesis 0, because he is writing of something God did *before* the foundation of the world.

Paul is saying that you and I were "spoken forth" out of the heart of God's love before the foundation of the world. That is a truth of radical significance. Here is the ultimate ground of our identity. You are a beloved child of God, spoken forth out of the heart of God's love before the foundation of the world. The union of a man and a woman that brought about your physical conception is only the secondary cause of your being. The primary center of your identity is the heart of God's love before the foundation of the world.

I heard a story a number of years ago that wonderfully illustrates this reality. I was speaking at an event where there was a couple with whom I was friends. They invited me to dinner one evening during this event. They also invited two or three others as well as a couple whom I did not know. During the course of the meal, someone asked the wife of this couple to share something of her spiritual pilgrimage. So she did.

She was the daughter of a prostitute. She was literally a job-related accident! She'd been raised by aunts, uncles, grandparents, even her mother from time to time, who continued to ply her trade. As a young teenager, she was drawn into a church youth group through her peer-group relationships, and there she discovered the love of God in Christ and responded to that love. When she graduated from high school, she went to a Christian college, and there she met a young man; they fell in love and were married. He was a good provider, he had a good job, they had a wonderful home and two lovely children. It seemed to me one of those "rags to riches" kind of stories.

Then she shared with us that her beautiful home, her wonderful marriage and her family were being destroyed because of her compulsive need to know who her father was. She was spending every ounce of energy and all the resources she could muster to try to find out who her father was. Of course, it was impossible. She would badger her mother, "Who were your clients nine months before I was born?" Her mother didn't have the slightest idea. There was just no way to learn who her father was.

Then she told us that one day she was standing at her kitchen sink, cleaning some dishes. She was alone. In the pain and anguish of her heart, her tears running down her face and dropping into the dishwater, she cried out, "Oh God, who is my father?"

She heard a voice say, "I am your Father."

She said the voice was so real she turned around to see who had sneaked into the kitchen behind her. No one was there.

She heard the voice again. "I am your Father, and I have always been your Father."

In that moment she was released from that obsessive need to know who her biological father had been. In that moment she discovered the truth of what Paul tells us about ourselves in Ephesians 1:4. She learned that, in spite of the strange dynamics surrounding her conception and birth, she was a person spoken forth out of the heart of God's love before the foundation of the world.

That is who we are.

We are not merely "spoken forth" out of the heart of God's love, however. We are spoken forth that we might be "holy and blameless before God in love." Our being (holy) and our doing (blameless) are to be the incarnation of a life lived in loving union with God.[1]

THE HORRIBLE PROBLEM OF THE FALSE SELF

Now we have a problem. We still have that old false self we have been discussing in the previous chapters. We are slow to realize, however, the hopeless state of our false self. Our false self objectifies itself over against God and, of course, over against others and the world. You might illustrate this for yourself with this exercise.

Clasp your hands together firmly. This represents life in loving union with God.

Unclasp your hands and stretch out your right arm fully to the side. When we become self-referenced beings, false selves, we loose our being from God's loving clasp and hold ourselves apart from God as a self-referenced being.

Our true self is found clasped in God's love. God has created us to be partakers of the divine nature, as Peter puts it (2 Pet 1:4), to find our wholeness in the very being of God, to be restored to fullness in the image of God, to live in loving union with God.

How then does our false self, the hand separated from God in its self-referenced life, get back into the clasp of God's love? Here is where we discover the radical nature of our lostness, our alienation, our separation from God. The very essence of our false self is that we are a self-referenced being. Any effort we make to try to get back into the clasp of God's love is a self-generated effort of the very nature that separates it from God. It is like trying to put together the positive poles of two powerful magnets. What happens? The closer they get together, the more they repel one another. Don't push this image too far because, you see, God does not repel us. The point is that the very essence of our false self makes us totally, utterly incapable of moving ourself back to our true center, of moving ourselves back into the context of our true wholeness, of returning to the clasp of God's love.

Our false self is hopelessly, unalterably imprisoned in its pervasively self-referenced way of being. There is no way out as far as our own resources and abilities are concerned. What then is the solution?

GOD'S RADICAL SOLUTION

Here is where we begin to understand the depth of God's cruciform love, grace and mercy toward us: "While we still were sinners [while we were still false selves] Christ died for us" (Rom 5:8 NRSV). Paul is saying that God comes to us *in our false self* in order to offer God's self to us to be our true life.

I believe the most profound image of this reality is found in Revelation 12. John has a vision of "a woman clothed with the sun, with the moon under her feet, and on her head a crown of twelve stars" (Rev 12:1 NRSV). This sounds sort of weird to us. What on earth is John seeing? In that period of time a person was known by their attributes. You could tell what social caste a person belonged to by the clothing worn. People with purple in their clothing were the uppermost class—the imperial family or senatorial families. If they wore red, then they belonged to the equestrian order—primarily lawyers and financiers, and so on.

You could also tell who deities were by their attributes. If you were walking down a street in Corinth and saw a male statue with a trident in his hand and dolphins at his feet, you knew it was Poseidon (or Neptune), the god of the sea. If you saw a female deity with a hunting cap, a bow and two hunting dogs by her side, you knew it was Artemis (or Diana), the goddess of the hunt.

John uses a well-known Jewish pool of images in order to convey the reality of his visionary experience. The problem is that these images are not at all common to us, so we see all sorts of weird things going on with Revelation that have little to do with what Revelation is all about.

The woman John sees is clothed with the sun. Throughout the Old Testament the images of brightness, fire and light are related to God. In Psalm 104:2, the psalmist says to God, "You have clothed yourself with light as with a garment." This suggests that the woman is God. She has the moon under her feet. Israel's worship is a lunar-based cycle. Note the references to new or full moons, festivals and sabbaths in the Old Testament.[2] (This is why Easter moves all over the calendar. Easter is the first Sunday after the first full moon after the vernal equinox, because Passover is the first full moon after the vernal equinox.) What we have here is a picture of God enthroned on the praises of Israel. Finally, the woman has a crown of twelve stars. Twelve, of course, represents the twelve tribes.[3] Israel is imaged as a crown in a couple of places in the Old Testament (Is 62:3; Zech 9:16). The imagery that John is using, therefore, indicates the woman is God. John sees that God, the woman, is just about ready to give birth, and in front of her is the dragon, Satan, who will devour the child when it is born. What a bizarre image!

The child is born and is immediately snatched up to God's throne. There are very few points in Revelation where most commentators agree, but they agree on this—the child is Jesus; this is the incarnation. Being snatched up, of course, is the ascension. Then where is the crucifixion? It is in the word *snatched.* The Greek word used means to take something that is in the possession of another. This indicates the dragon got the child. Here is the crucifixion.

John is seeing a profound reality. The cross is not something God did around A.D.30 on a hillside outside

Jerusalem. John is seeing that *the cross is a revelation of who God is in the very core of God's being.* This scene appears in John's vision before Satan's rebellion in heaven several verses later. This is why in chapter 13 John speaks of the Lamb, John's primary image for Jesus, as the Lamb that was slain before the foundation of the world.[4]

You are probably thinking, *Wait a minute, John. The Lamb was slain in Jerusalem in A.D.30.* John would reply, "No, no, no; that's just simply the historical incarnation or manifestation of the deeper reality of who God is." The cross is the revelation in history of the very essence of God's nature as cruciform love. God is one who, in the very essence of God's being, comes to us in our false self, who enters into our false self to liberate us from its destructive bondage from which we cannot liberate ourselves, and to enable us to be restored in the fullness of God's very own image in loving union with God.

Go back to the illustration of the clasped and separated hands (especially if you are still sitting there with your

right hand stretched out to your side!).
While it is impossible for our false self
to restore us into the clasp of God's
love, God has clasped our false self in
cruciform love so that our false self
might be crucified with Christ and we
might be raised with him to life in
loving union with God.

We have to ask at this point: "How
does our false self relate to our Christ
self, our true self? What is the
relationship between these two?" We
usually think of these as polar
opposites, and, to be sure, there is a
sense in which this is true. Our false
self certainly is not our Christ self; we
are not in loving union with God even
though we may be a highly developed
religious false self. The relationship
between these two selves is a divine
mystery. Christ dwells in the depths of
our false self as the crucified one, yet
at the same time as the risen Lord and
our new life, our Christ self.

In the light of this mystery, let's
look at some passages that might give
us help in understanding. In 2
Corinthians 4:6-7 Paul writes:

For it is the God who said, "Let light shine out of darkness," who has shone in our hearts to give the light of the knowledge of the glory of God in the face of Jesus Christ.

But we have this treasure in clay jars, so that it may be made clear that this extraordinary power belongs to God and does not come from us. (NRSV)

Paul implies that our false self is darkness and that God becomes manifest in this darkness through Christ, who brings into the darkness of our false self the consciousness of God's very nature ("glory").[5] Paul then makes it clear that this experience of Christ within us is not something generated by our false self even though it takes place in the context of the false self. In 2 Corinthians 4:10-11, Paul draws the conclusion from this experience:

...always carrying in the body the death of Jesus, so that the life of Jesus may also be made visible in our bodies. For while we live, we are always being given up to death for Jesus' sake, so that the life of

Jesus may be made visible in our mortal flesh. (NRSV)

Paul says here that the death of Christ is operative in our false self so that our Christ life might become manifest out of this false self. As we allow our false self to be given up to death for Jesus' sake, to be crucified with Christ (Gal 2:19), to lose itself for Christ's sake (Mt 10:39), then the life of Jesus may become visible in us, a life of loving union with God.

This seems to be precisely what Paul writes to the Romans:

> For you did not receive a spirit of slavery to fall back into fear, but you have received a spirit of adoption. When we cry, "Abba! Father!" it is that very Spirit bearing witness with our spirit that we are children of God, and if children, then heirs, heirs of God and joint heirs with Christ—if, in fact, we suffer with him so that we may also be glorified with him. (Rom 8:15-17 NRSV)

After powerfully affirming our restored status as beloved children, Paul elaborates on the purpose of that restoration—to be heirs of God and joint heirs of Christ,[6] in other words, to be restored to wholeness in the image of God (heirs of God), to become Christlike (heirs of Christ).[7] Paul then gives us the condition on which this occurs: "if, in fact, we suffer with him so that we may also be glorified with him." The false self must be crucified with Christ if we are to become glorified, or have the same nature with Christ.

Paul is saying that entering into the core of our false self with Christ is a cruciform experience. This is where the cross exists for us. The cross is grounded in the core of our false self, and it is by entering into the core of our false self that we experience the cruciform love of God in Christ. When we embrace the cross there, in our false self, we release that false self to the cross, to Christ, to the crucified One. In that release we begin to experience the power of his resurrection raising us out of the deadness of the false self into the wholeness of life in the image of Christ, life in loving union with God. That is, as we suffer with him, we are also glorified with him.

This is what Jesus was talking about when he said, "If any wish to come after me, let them deny their self, take up their cross, and follow me" (Mt 16:24). Once again, this doesn't mean giving up candy for Lent. It means the abandonment of our false self, the relinquishment of our whole, pervasive, self-referenced structure of being. Our cross and Jesus' cross are united. His cross is the presence of his love at the core of our false self.

We see this imaged in a beautiful way in John's vision. The Laodicean church was a mess (Rev 3:14-22). This church was an archetypal religious false self. Their self-evaluation is: "We are rich, we have prospered, we need nothing." Jesus' evaluation of them is: "You are wretched, pitiable, poor, blind, and naked" (v. 17 NRSV). They thought they had it all together. What they had done, however, was to retain the false self values of Laodicea. They had allowed the world to set their agenda and to form their understanding of themselves as the body of Christ. To this epitome of the religious false self Jesus says an interesting thing: "I stand at the door and knock; if anyone hears my voice and opens the door, I will come in to them and eat with them, and they with me" (v. 20).

Play with this image for a minute. What is the door on which Jesus knocks? It is the door of our false self. It is those places in our life where we have shut God out and enclosed ourself within our self-referenced structure of being, where we are imprisoned in our false self. But notice the movement here. God doesn't call us to clean up our act and come out to have a good relationship with God. God calls us to open the door so that God can come in, come into our false self. God's cruciform love seeks to enter into the depths of our darkness, our sin, our deadness, our brokenness, our bondage. What will God do when God comes in? "I will eat with them and they with me." The word that John uses here for "eat" is the word that is used in the New Testament for the Lord's Supper.[8] When God enters into our false self, it is the sacrament of God's presence, another image of the cross. God comes into the core of our self-referenced being. God comes to bring light into our darkness, cleansing into our sin, life into our deadness, healing into our brokenness, liberation into our bondage; to nurture us there into wholeness in the very image of God. But to open that door is to acknowledge our false self and to allow God to come in, knowing that when the love of God encounters the false self, it is always a cruciform encounter for God and for us.

How do we do this? How do we open the door? In fact, what is that door? We might think of the door as any aspect of our false self that prevents God from being God in our life on God's terms. It may be a habit that holds us in its destructive bondage, an attitude that deforms our way of living, a perception that warps our view of others, a pattern of relationships with others that is destructive to both them and us, a way of reacting to circumstances that hinders us, a cancerous resentment whose poison is eating away the vitals of our being. Whatever the door may be for us, it is something to which our false self has become attached and in which we are finding something of our identity, meaning, value or purpose. The hinges of this door are mounted in the depths of our being. To put it simply, the door is something we love more than we love God. To open this door is to breech the wall of our false self, to release our possessive grip that holds the door closed, to respond to the cruciform love of the nail-scarred hand that knocks, to receive the nurture into Christlikeness that is offered.

Let's say, for example, one of your doors is a long-held, deep-seated resentment at someone who has wronged you. The anger, the bitterness, the pain of what they did have birthed dreams of revenge, which you have fed and nurtured so many times they have now become woven into your very being. Part of your false self has become identified by this resentment. How do you open this door? *By forgiving the one who wronged you!* [9] This is taking up the cross. Forgiveness is a death to your false self and its righteous indignation, its justified rationale for revenge, its fondling of the resentment. This death is extremely painful; everything in your false self screams out against it; this is truly dying with Christ. The instant you even touch this door of resentment with the faintest desire to open it by forgiveness, Christ is present to enable you to open it fully. He comes in, and as you continue to rely on him to enable you to forgive, you begin to experience his cruciform love nurturing you in that love, healing the hurt, removing the resentment, flushing away the bitterness until one day you realize that Christ's love and forgiveness have become incarnate in you for the one who wronged you. Your Christ self has come to life!

Paul describes this dying with Christ and being made whole in his likeness in another way in his testimony in Philippians 3:4-14. We have already seen how Paul discovered that his perfect holiness, the religiosity of his false self, was worth no more than a pile of dog's droppings.[10] Paul abandoned his religious false self, "in order that I may know him and the power of his resurrection and the partnership[11] of his sufferings; being conformed to his death, if somehow I might attain the resurrection from the dead" (vv. 10-11). Notice Paul's structure. Knowing Christ entails both suffering and resurrection. He begins with resurrection: "that I might know him and the power of his resurrection," and ends with his desire to partake of the resurrection. In between, Paul points to the partnership of Christ's suffering and being conformed with Christ's death.[12] Paul is indicating that our resurrection into this new life, our true self, our Christ self, has its center in our partnership with Christ's suffering and conformity with his death. This means allowing the presence of Christ to plumb the depths of our false self and to abandon our false self to the cruciform love of God.

THE CONTEXT FOR BECOMING A TRUE SELF

Opening the door of resentment through forgiveness is but one step on our deeper journey into Christlikeness. Is there a larger context in which such focused disciplines take place? Is there perhaps a more comprehensive perspective or orientation within which we open each of the doors of our false self to God's cleansing, healing, liberation and transformation? There is, and it is to this Paul turns our attention.

Having given us a stark warning about the destructive dangers of the religious false self in Colossians 2:20-23, Paul begins to instruct us on how we are nurtured into Christlikeness, into a life of loving union with God.

Paul begins Colossians 3:1-4 with "Since you have been raised with Christ..." We are immediately confronted with a vital element in the deeper journey. In Colossians 2:20, Paul wrote, "Since you died with Christ..." using the active form of the verb, indicating that dying with Christ is something we are actively involved in. We must choose to be crucified with Christ; we must "take up our cross"; we must acknowledge and relinquish our false self; we are the ones who "open the door." In Colossians 3:1, however, Paul shifts to the passive voice for the verb, indicating that resurrection with Christ is something in which we play no active role. This is God's work, done in God's way. This is what makes abandoning our religious false self so difficult. We would perhaps be much more inclined to abandon our false self if we could be assured that what replaces it will be acceptable to us, be compatible with our desires, further our plans, fulfill our purposes and meet our agenda.

We might be more likely to "die with Christ" if we had some control over what being raised with Christ looks like. We may have an even deeper resistance arising from the uncertainty of whether there will even be a resurrection if we die with Christ. How can I even be sure, if I relinquish my false self, that there will be anything to replace it? Paul will give us the answer to this shortly. At this point we can only note that relinquishing our false self for Christ's sake is an act of radical abandonment. It isn't like the trapeze artist who lets go of the bar as the other bar reaches the proper position for the transfer. It is letting go of the bar of our false self in a total trust that God will provide for us the bar of a new being even though we have no idea what that will be. I am sure you realize how difficult this is. Jesus' images of cutting off a hand or plucking out an eye come to mind (Mt 5:29-30). After all, we are being asked to relinquish the only self we have ever known, to literally lose our self.

How do we do this? Ultimately, this is a movement of love. Loving union with God in Christ is the culmination of a journey which we are offered in the cruciform love of God that penetrates the darkness of our false self; a journey that begins with our response of loving abandonment to that cruciform love.[13] Our loving response is a movement from the very center of our being. Paul now turns our attention to this movement.

"Since you have been raised with Christ," Paul says, "strive for the things that are above, where Christ is, seated at the right hand of God. Orient your entire being toward the things above, not the things upon the earth" (Col 3:1-2). The crucial terms here are "strive" and "orient your entire being."

The focus of our striving and the orientation of our being are on Christ in unity with God. Such striving and such orientation have but one true driving motive—loving abandonment to God, a hungering and thirsting for the things of God.

Paul urges us to strive because our false self is deeply embedded in our status quo. The habitual inertia of our self-referenced mode of being keeps us moving always in the same direction. Our false self unconsciously enters into every relationship and meets every situation out of our deeply habituated self-referenced orientation. It requires striving to redirect the trajectory of our journey.

Striving alone, however, is not sufficient. After all, the Colossians had certainly been striving for holiness as religious false selves, engaged in rigorous religiosity, self-generated humility, even severe ascetic practices. Our striving must be part of a deeper movement, an inner paradigm shift, a reorientation at the core of our being. When Paul says, "Orient your entire being," he uses a Greek term usually rendered "set your mind." This, however, misses the deeper dimensions of the term. We can grasp Paul's use of the term in Philippians 2:5-11, where to *have the mind* of Christ" is to be in the same kind of radical abandonment and total availability to God that Jesus manifested. Paul uses the term to portray a profound inner restructuring of our being. He calls for a shift from our pervasively self-referenced mode of being to a radically Christ-referenced mode of being.

Paul illustrates this shift by contrasting "things above" with "things on earth." Since the "things above" are "where Christ is, seated at the right hand of God," Paul obviously is calling us to root our lives firmly in God's realm of being and to strive to incarnate its values, its perspectives, its mode of being in our lives in the world. "Things on earth" would represent a realm of being devoid of Christ and God, the realm of our false self with its thoroughly self-referenced values, perspectives and mode of being in the world.

It would be easy for us to assume, reading Colossians 3:1-2, that the life of loving union with God is a matter of our effort. We simply reorient our inner being and strive to live our lives out of that new orientation. How would this be any different from our religious false self? It wouldn't. It would be the epitome of the religious false self. This is why Paul hastens to add verses 3-4.

Paul begins Colossians 3:3 with a Greek particle, usually translated "for," which is used to introduce the reason for what precedes. It is clear that the only valid context for our inner reorientation and striving is the fact that "you have died, and your life is hidden with Christ in God" (NRSV). Paul is speaking here of the profound reality of what God has done in Christ. In the death of Christ the entirety of the nature of our false self was confirmed as dead.[14] This is why Paul consistently portrays life apart from God as death:

> You were *dead* through the trespasses and sins in which you once lived…. Even when we were *dead* through our trespasses, [God]

made us alive together with Christ. (Eph 2:1-2, 5 NRSV, emphasis added)

Rise from the *dead,//*and Christ will shine on you. (Eph 5:14 NRSV, emphasis added)

And when you were *dead* in trespasses, ... God made you alive together with him. (Col 2:13 NRSV, emphasis added)

For Paul, any striving of our false self to be holy, any self-generated restructuring of our false self, no matter how religious, is merely changing the window display in the same old store. Our false self, even our religious false self, is dead.

Fortunately, there is the rest of the story: "Your life has been hidden with Christ in God" (Col 3:3). Here we come to mystery. First, this life, whatever it is, is not something we have generated. It is something God has already hidden with Christ. Second, the root of this life is not grounded in us; it's grounded with Christ in God. Paul seems to be saying that in the cross of Jesus, God has done two things: (1) God has entered into the entirety of our false self and confirmed it as dead, and (2) in the core of that deadness God has planted Christ as the seed of a true life in loving union with God. Paul has stated this another way in Galatians: "I have been crucified with Christ; it is no longer I who live but Christ who lives in me" (Gal 2:19-20). When we awaken to this indwelling reality at the core of our being and turn from the deadness of our false self to be embraced by the indwelling love of Christ, our "life ... hidden with Christ in God" begins to live itself forth in us. We begin to see ourselves and others through the eyes of Christ. We begin to have the mind of Christ (1 Cor 2:16) as we deal with the circumstances and situations of our life. Our life begins to be shaped by kingdom values.

Perhaps the mystical nature of this reality is seen most clearly in Paul's prayer in Ephesians 3:16-19:

> I pray *that* according to the riches of God's very nature, [1] you may be strengthened with power through God's Spirit in your inner being, *that* [2] Christ may dwell in your hearts through faith, *that* [3]

you, being rooted and grounded in love, may have the power *to comprehend* with all the saints what is the breadth and length and height and depth, *to know* the love of Christ that surpasses knowledge, *that* [4] you may be filled with all the fullness of God.

Paul's prayer is not just theological, it is ontological; Paul is dealing with the mystical reality of the life that "has been hidden with Christ in God." This is the unalterable ground of the Christian life, the profound reality of Christian experience, the essence of life in loving union with God.

Paul expresses in four movements the single reality of loving union with God. First, loving union with God is being strengthened with power by God's indwelling presence—the Holy Spirit—in our innermost being. Our false self and religious false self are so profoundly habituated to being in control of our life that the reality of a life completely under God's control is unfathomable. At best, the Holy Spirit is perceived by our religious false self as a resource for fulfilling its own agenda. Jesus, as well as Paul and the other New Testament writers, makes it clear, however, that the Holy Spirit is the source, cause and power of life in loving union with God. "What is born of the flesh is flesh, and what is born of the Spirit is spirit" (Jn 3:6 NRSV). "It is the Spirit that gives life; the flesh is useless" (Jn 6:63 NRSV). "God's love has been poured into our hearts through the Holy Spirit that has been given to us" (Rom 5:5 NRSV). "By this we know that we abide in him and he in us, because he has given us of his Spirit" (1 Jn 4:13 NRSV).

Paul makes it clear that the alternative to our false self—life according to the flesh—is "life according to the Spirit."

For God has done what the law, weakened by the flesh, could not do: by sending his own Son in the likeness of sinful flesh, and to deal with sin, he condemned sin in the flesh, so that the just requirement of the law might be fulfilled in us, who walk not according to the *flesh* but according to the *Spirit.* For those who live according to the flesh *set their minds on the things of the flesh,* but those who live according to the Spirit *set their minds on the things of the Spirit.* To *set the mind on the flesh* is death, but to *set the mind on the Spirit* is life and peace.[15] (Rom 8:3-6 NRSV, emphasis added)

The "just requirement of the law" might well be understood as a life lived in loving union with God, a life in which God's presence touches others. Such a life can only result from being transformed and empowered by the Spirit for such Christlike living.

Paul succinctly describes the work of the Spirit in such transformation:

Now the Lord is the Spirit, and where the Spirit of the Lord is, there is freedom. And all of us, with unveiled faces, seeing the glory of the Lord as though reflected in a mirror, are being transformed into the same image from one degree of glory to another; for this comes from the Lord, the Spirit. (2 Cor 3:17-18 NRSV)

Note that the Spirit liberates us from the veil of our false self, which separates us from God.[16] We are enabled by the Spirit to behold something of the very essence of God's being (glory) without the distortions of the darkened perspectives of our false self. Through such "seeing the glory of the Lord" the Spirit engenders a process of transformation of our very being into the image of God, from the debased nature (glory) of our false self to the restored nature (glory) of our true identity as persons created in the image of God.

To "be strengthened with power through God's Spirit in your inner being" (Eph 3:16), therefore, is to be nurtured by the Holy Spirit into a life of loving union with God, a life of increasing Christlikeness. We must always remember, however, that such a life is always for the sake of others. Christlikeness is a life of utter abandonment to God in love and, at the same time, total availability to God for others. "To each is given the manifestation of the Spirit for the common good" (1 Cor 12:7 NRSV). To "be strengthened with power through God's Spirit in your inner being" is to be empowered to be broken bread and poured-out wine for the life of the world. This is an integral part of the "life hidden with Christ in God."

Second, loving union with God is the indwelling presence of Christ in our hearts. Again Paul is not speaking theologically but ontologically. The indwelling presence of Christ in us is not merely a theological concept, it is a vital, intimate, relational reality at the very core of our being. Paul stresses this profound reality incessantly.[17]

Anyone who does not have the Spirit of Christ does not belong to him. But if *Christ is in you ...* (Rom 8:9-10)

He is not weak in dealing with you, but *is powerful in you.* (2 Cor 13:3)

Examine yourselves to see whether you are living in the faith. Test yourselves. Do you not realize that *Jesus Christ is in you?* (2 Cor 13:5)

My little children, for whom I am again in the pain of childbirth until *Christ is formed in you ...* (Gal 4:19)

...Christ in you, the hope of glory. (Col 1:27)

The following are a sample of John's attestation to the mysterious reality of the indwelling presence of Christ that Jesus calls us to.

On that day you will know that I am in my Father, and you in me, and *I in you.* (Jn 14:20)

Abide in me as *I abide in you....* Those who abide in me and *I in them* bear much fruit, because apart from me you can do nothing. (Jn 15:4-5)

The glory that you have given me I have given them, so that they may be one, as we are one, *I in them* and you in me, that they may become completely one, so that the world may know that you have sent me and have loved them even as you have loved me. (Jn 17:22-23)

Perhaps the most profound expression of the mystery of the indwelling presence of Christ is in Jesus' words: "Those who eat my flesh and drink my blood abide in me, and *I in them*" (Jn 6:56). When Jesus' hearers had as much difficulty with this word as we do, he replied, "The words that I have spoken to you are spirit and life" (Jn 6:63). Might it not be possible that Jesus is indicating the necessity of our involvement in his death? The first movement of Christ's indwelling love is to enter into the death of our false self. Only when we enter that movement and participate in that death can the second movement of being raised to life with Christ occur.

Christ dwelling in our hearts through faith, therefore, is a process of entering, with Christ, ever more fully into the labyrinth of our false self and suffering with him in the death of our self-referenced being, through which we are raised up with him out of that death into a life of loving union with God. This too is an integral part of the "life hidden with Christ in God."

Third, and the crux of it all, loving union with God is a life "rooted and grounded in love" (Eph 3:17); rooted, first, in the cruciform love of God for us at the heart of our false self, and grounded, second, in our response of a loving abandonment to God, which allows God to be God in our life on

God's terms. The experience of God's nature as cruciform love, as an unfathomable divine self-abandonment, calls us to a concomitant abandonment of self in love. We become "rooted and grounded" in a love of mutual self-abandonment.

Such a union of love, however, awakens us to "the breadth, length, height, and depth" (Eph 3:18) of God's true being as well as our own. We begin to experience the mystery that God's self is not in any way diminished in God's unfathomable self-abandonment but is fully manifest, and that our true self, created in God's image, is engendered by God only through the abandonment of our false self. To "*comprehend* ... the breadth and length and height and depth" is, as Paul explains by his appositional phrase, to "*know* the love of Christ that surpasses knowledge" (NRSV, emphasis added).[18] How do we know something that surpasses knowledge? It is the experience of loving union with a God whom we will never be able to grasp with our minds and understanding. It is experiencing that we love and are loved by an infinite love. Thomas Merton says of this passage:

> The result of this indwelling of Christ and of the Holy Spirit is the overflowing fullness of new life, of charity, divine love, and a spiritual comprehension of the mystery of God's life within us in all its dimensions, through the experience of Christ's love for us "which surpasses all understanding."[19]

This, perhaps, is an integral and essential part of the "hiddenness" of the life "hidden with Christ in God."

Fourth, loving union with God is being "filled with all the fullness of God" (Eph 3:19). Life "hidden with Christ in God" is just such a life. It is, as Paul says, "A new creation, where old things are passed away and, behold, all things become new" (2 Cor 5:17). This is the epitome of the life of loving union with God. The union is not simply a tangential contact of two beings, a "surface" touching. It is a merging of our being with God and God with us, our true humanness in God's image as revealed in Christ.

Of course, Paul in no way infers that we can somehow "contain" the infinite God within the parameters of our finite being. To be "filled with all the fullness of God" is to experience God as the life of our life. Perhaps a terribly inadequate illustration might provide an image of this reality.

Illustration 4.1.

If you think of the closed cone as representing our finite human existence, the bottom open-ended cone would represent God. If we choose to live with the center of our being at some point other than in God, we are a false self. To the extent we are centered in God, however, all the infinite reality of the God cone becomes both the context and the essential content of our life. We might also think of the cone of our existence being drawn ever deeper into

God so that God increasingly becomes our life in the world.

There is another way to think of being filled with all the fullness of God. Most of us think of a vessel of some sort filled to the top. If this is the case, then to be filled with all the fullness of God is to have our being filled to the top with God, as though God were something we possessed. Consider this image:

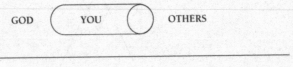

Illustration 4.2.

Think of your self as a pipe, open at both ends. At one end of your pipe is a flange specifically designed for loving union with God. The other end of your pipe has a flange specifically designed for loving service for others. When the connection is made at both ends of your pipe, then the presence of God moves through you to others. In that process three things happen. You are filled with all the fullness of God, you experience your life hidden with Christ in God, and you experience your true self, your Christ self.

Paul reminds us that this life is "hidden." We would love to understand everything about who we are, who we truly are. We would love to have it all in place and under our control. But this life hidden with Christ in God is hidden from us. When we begin to push into the core of who we truly are, we encounter mystery, because the core of who we really are somehow becomes enmeshed with who God really is, and we can never get our minds around that reality.

We would love to know who we are at the very core of our being so we could grab our bootstraps and get to work and actualize it. It is our false self, our religious false self that has to have this kind of control. We can't stand the ambiguity of not knowing what God is going to make of us. Here is where you will have the greatest difficulty dying to your false self and allowing God's cruciform love to truly plumb the depths of your self-referenced structure of being, particularly your religious false self.

Paul is not finished. He says, "Whenever Christ, your life, should become manifest, then you also will be manifested with him in glory" (Col 3:4). Paul has two subjects in this part of the sentence: "Christ," and "your life."[20] This is another way of saying "your life has been hidden with Christ in God." In this mystical union with Christ in love, Christ becomes our true life or, as Paul says, "It is Christ who lives in me" (Gal 2:20 NRSV).

"Whenever Christ, your life, should become manifest," Paul says, "you also will be manifested with him in glory." Paul is not simply speaking eschatologically here. Paul is not talking about some distant event, he is talking about an essential dimension of daily life. Paul is saying whenever we allow Christ truly to indwell us, allow the Holy Spirit to transformingly empower us, allow the fullness of God to be the context and content of our life in the world, then who we truly are becomes manifest in its Christlikeness. We will "appear with him in glory," (Col 3:4 NRSV) in the very nature of who Christ is.[21] Paul's "whenever" points to any relationship, any situation or circumstance in our daily life. When, in that moment, we live in loving union with God, our life becomes a place where others experience the presence of God's love, mercy and grace touching their lives with cleansing, healing and liberating transformation.

Christ (our life) can become manifest in very mundane, common, everyday events. Several years ago I was invited to speak at a camp meeting. I was met at the airport by one of the camp staff, and as we drove to the camp, this person told me about a woman who came to the camp every year. She was a deeply wounded, very troubled woman, and the staff person told me to have nothing to do with her. I began to wonder just what kind of situation I had gotten myself into. I had presumed that I was invited to be at this meeting so that Christ might be able to touch the lives of those there through the ministry he would give me.

After I spoke the first evening, this woman approached me—she had been described well so I could recognize her—and asked if she might talk with me. I ignored the advice I had been given and agreed to meet with her after lunch the next day. The next morning, as I was accustomed to doing, I went for a walk on the road that ran beside the camp. It was a one-lane dirt road, and a mile up the road was a crossroad where I would turn and go back to the camp. As I approached the crossroad, I noticed in the distance a person walking toward the road I was on. But he or she was too far away to identify.

As I approached the camp on my return, I noticed a fast-food bag with a cup, a French fries container, and napkins discarded in the ditch beside the road. As I walked by God told me, "Pick up the trash."

Once I recovered from the surprise of this unmistakable word from God, my religious false self kicked into gear. I responded, "I don't do trash." After all, I was the vice president of a seminary, a senior professor, a speaker at this camp meeting. I didn't come here to pick trash out of the ditches. So I walked on.

God said again, "Pick up the trash."

Realizing that God was serious about this, I took him at his word (Is 1:18) and decided to reason with him. "God,"

I said, "This stuff is biodegradable. Rain on it; you can handle this." I continued on my way.

"Pick up the trash!"

I turned, retraced my path back to the trash and picked it up. There was a dumpster beside the gate of the camp, and I tossed the trash in and returned to my room.

"God, what was that all about?"

Silence. God had been unmistakably clear out there on the road, but now—nothing.

After lunch the woman came for her appointment. When she had taken a seat, she said, "May I say something to you?"

"Sure," I replied. After all, this was her appointment, her agenda.

"I was walking behind you on the road this morning." (She had been the person I had seen on the crossroad when I turned.) "When I saw you turn around and pick up that trash, I knew you were real."

In that act of reluctant obedience, God had somehow manifested something of Christlikeness to her. This opened the door for the Lord to minister to her deeply and, I learned later, in cleansing, healing, liberating ways that transformed her life.

Reflecting on the nature of our self and identity in the light of what Paul says about the life hidden with Christ in God and manifested in Christlikeness, it would seem our true self-identity is something completely out of our control. Our part is to be completely abandoned to God in love and fully available to God for others. In the nothingness of a self utterly devoid of self-referenced dynamics, totally devoted to God for others, in the exigency of the nothingness that stands between God and the other, God forms us as a self who manifests something of God's presence to the other. At the same time, God is mysteriously present in the other for us and shapes our self-identity in that relationship.

We tend to perceive our self-identity as a possession for which we are responsible, an entity separate from God and the other that has to take on multiple levels of "Christian" coloration and then act it out in relationships and situations. This is the way of the religious false self. The deeper dimensions of Paul's statement that our life is hidden with Christ in God, as well as his later claim that Christ is all and in all (Col 3:11), introduces us to the mystery of a Christ-referenced self. Our Christ-referenced self is what God, through the Holy Spirit, engenders in us in the context of the relationships and situations of our daily life. Thus every situation and every relationship provide ever new settings and opportunities for God to actualize our true selfidentity. While there will, of course, be an ever deepening stability in the nature of our true self-identity, it will never be an entity to which we attach ourselves. The moment we attach ourselves to any point of this development, we again become self-referenced and our self-identity becomes a commodity we possess and employ.

One of the deepest mysteries of a Christ-referenced life is that only by losing all, by becoming utterly devoid of all self-referenced dynamics, by becoming "nothingness" do we gain all, do we gain a life whose "joys are ravishing, its peace profound, its humility the deepest, its power world-shaking, its love enveloping, its simplicity that of a trusting child."[22] We enter into wholeness and fullness of life in loving union with God for the sake of others. The most difficult part of all is that we can't become devoid of all self-referenced dynamics for the purpose of gaining this life of loving union with God. If we do so, we act again in a self-referenced manner, seeking to gain God for ourselves, making the image of God something to be grasped.

This reality calls us to the discipline that the classical Christian journey has called "contemplation." This is the practice of stilling ourselves before God, moving ever deeper into the core of our being and simply offering ourselves to God in totally vulnerable love. The daily disciplined offering of ourselves to God in this way can be used by God to lead us into a life of amazing centeredness, a life through which God lives in us for others. In the words of Thomas Kelly:

>What is here urged are secret
>habits of unceasing orientation of

the deeps of our being about the Inward Light, ways of conducting our inward life so that we are perpetually bowed in worship, while we are also very busy in the world of daily affairs....

A Practicing Christian must above all be one who practices the perpetual return of the soul into the inner sanctuary, who brings the world into its Light and rejudges it, who brings the Light into the world with all its turmoil and its fitfulness and recreates it.[23]

We will look at this discipline in more detail in chapter seven.

CONCLUSION

We have seen the awesome reality of how God relates our false self to our true self, our Christ self. God's cruciform love indwells our false self to liberate us from its destructive and dehumanizing bondage. God's resurrection love indwells our false self to raise us from its death, to nurture us toward wholeness in loving union with God in Christ, to enable us to be in the world those in whom Christ lives for others. The question now is, "What do we need to do?" How can this profound reality become actualized in our life? Paul leads us into the difficult answers.

Here are some probes you may want to use to reflect on what we have been discussing.

- Do you understand God "over against" your false self or in its depths?
- Is the cross something God did or who God is?
- Having reflected on the first two probes, does this change your understanding of yourself and of God?
- What does it mean to be hidden with Christ in God?
- Where do you go with all this as far as your life is concerned?

5

ABANDONING THE FALSE SELF

Gracious and loving God, whose cruciform love penetrates into the depths of my being, whose resurrection power awaits to raise me out of my deadness into loving union with you and transformed living in the world, help me as I consider the disciplines of abandonment of the false self to hear deep within the voice of cruciform love calling me to come and die, and in that dying to find transformed life. I ask this in the name of the one who died and rose again, Jesus my Lord, who lives and reigns with you and the Holy Spirit, one God, now and forever. Amen.

How are we to enter into the fullness of that life "hidden with Christ in God?" Paul and the mothers and fathers of our spiritual tradition know only one way: the abandonment of vices and the appropriation of virtues. In Colossians 2:20—3:17, after contrasting the religious false self (2:20-23) with the life hidden with Christ in God (3:1-4), Paul turns to the abandonment of vices (3:5-11) and the appropriation of virtues (3:12-17). Both become means of grace by which God enables us to live in the world a life hidden with Christ in God.

Now, after so rigorously denouncing the self-referenced efforts of our religious false self in Colossians 2:20-23, it may seem that Paul is resorting to the same kind of efforts. You will see, however, that this is far from the truth. It will become evident that in his call for the abandonment of the vices Paul draws us into the deep inner dynamics of our false self from which the vices emerge and urges that we put to death these dynamics.

Paul's exhortation uses two lists of vices. These are not, however, simply a collection of ten vices Paul picked at random from a larger list of vices. The lists are very carefully crafted and closely integrated. The first list begins with outward behavior, "fornication," and moves through the inner processes behind the behavior to the deep inner ground of the entire list, "the covetousness which is idolatry" (Col 3:5). The second list begins with the inner processes, "anger, wrath, malice," and moves to the outward behavior, "abusive speech from your mouth" (Col 3:8). Linking the two lists at their center in the inner being is Paul's statement about the "wrath of God," which comes as a result of these things (Col 3:6-7). Let's look first at these verses, which bind the two lists together.

THE WRATH OF GOD

We should note that when Paul says, "the wrath of God is coming on account of these things" (v. 6), he is using a present tense verb. The wrath of God is a present experience for those engaged in a way of life characterized by the two lists. We tend to think of the wrath of God as the mean, punitive, vindictive, vengeful, retributive action of an offended deity. Perhaps an illustration might help you frame the wrath of God in a new perspective.

You are probably sitting or standing or lying comfortably as you read this because you are in perfect harmony with the law of gravity. Now what if the place where you are reading happened to be in the rooftop garden of a penthouse in a skyscraper? When the time comes for you to put this book aside and go to the restaurant down the street for dinner, what if, rather than taking the elevator, you decide simply to step off the edge of the roof? Does gravity suddenly become mean, punitive, vindictive, vengeful, retributive? Of course not! It simply continues to be gravity, and you quickly experience the deadly consequences of placing your life out of harmony with it.

Now, how does this relate to the wrath of God? We are created to find our fullness of life in loving union with God. When we live in such a relationship, our lives are integrated; we possess a deep inner stability and experience wholeness. When, however, we step out of that loving union with God, when we rebel against this essential reality of our being, we begin to experience the disintegration, instability and brokenness that result from uprooting our lives from their true center. God's relationship with us doesn't change. God continues to be the One whose love enfolds and indwells us. Stepping out of that relationship creates the radical disruptions in our being. The pain and suffering those disruptions bring into our lives we call the "wrath of God." By his use of this image Paul is simply reiterating what he said about our religious false selves in Colossians 2:22; all of our self-referenced efforts at holiness are "perishing with use." Our false self is an inherently destructive mode of being.

Paul then adds, "You all once walked in this kind of life when you were living in such ways" (Col 3:7). By applying these lists to all his readers, Paul makes it clear that we aren't dealing with vices that apply to a select few within the audience. It would be so easy for us to look at these lists and think, *Well, these don't apply to me.* Paul is describing the essential dynamics of all false selves, yours and mine included.

OUR BROKEN SEXUALITY

Paul's lists are introduced with the call to "Put to death the members upon the earth" (Col 3:5). There is an interesting interplay in Paul's terms for "put to death." The verb used here appears only twice in Paul's writings, here and in Romans 4:19. Paul's favorite verb for "put to death" is a word meaning "to kill," which is used everywhere else (forty-two times). The term Paul uses here denotes removing the life from something, to stop giving life to it, to stop energizing it, to stop animating it.

We are to cease giving life to "the members upon the earth." In the previous section (Col 3:1-4) we saw that "things upon the earth" are the antitheses of "things above, where Christ is." Obviously Paul is calling us to drain the life from all aspects of the self-referenced structures of our false self.

Paul then gives us one of the primary structures of our false self: "Fornication, immorality, lust, evil passion and the covetousness, which is idolatry" (Col 3:5). The focus of this list is broken sexuality. Paul uses *fornication* to denote aberrant sexual behavior, especially as the antithesis of the behavior of a life hidden with Christ in God—"The body is not for fornication but for the Lord" (1 Cor 6:13). Fornication is one of the primary "works of the flesh" (Gal 5:19), that is, works of our false self. It is interesting to note that when the mothers and fathers of our Christian spiritual tradition wrestle with the deepest dimensions of the false self, they frequently reduce those dimensions to broken sexuality and violence (the focus of Paul's second list in Col 3:8). Henri Nouwen puts it this way:

> We need silence in our lives. We even desire it. But when we enter into silence we encounter a lot of inner noises, often so disturbing that a busy and distracting life seems preferable to a time of silence. Two disturbing "noises" present themselves quickly in our silence: the noise of lust and the noise of anger.[1]

This is seconded by Aelred Squire: "Speaking in the most broad and general terms, the two basic forces in connection with which our life manifests itself are those of love and aggression."[2] It isn't too extreme to say that two of the greatest problems in Western culture today are broken sexuality and violence.

Why is this? Our sexuality is a profoundly integral aspect of our creation in the image of God. Sexuality is present at the very heart of human existence: "Let us make humans in our own image and likeness.... So God created humans in God's image, in the image of God God created them, male and female God created them" (Gen 1:26-27). Femaleness and maleness, therefore, are an integral part of our being created in the image of God. As such, our sexuality finds its proper place only when our lives are in loving union with God. When our maleness and femaleness are in loving union with God, they fulfill their proper role as the locus where the love, compassion, creativity and caring of God become incarnate in us for the sake of others.

In the self-referenced structures of our false self, however, our sexuality becomes the primary means by which we seek to manipulate others and the world according to our own agenda. Males have their own special ways of manipulating others, and females have theirs. Male manipulation tends to be aggressive and domineering, enforcing control. Female manipulation tends to be more subtle, more subversive, exploiting the strength of others for their own purposes. Instead of our maleness and femaleness being a means of God's grace in the lives of others, they become a means for our false self to impose itself on others in coercive, controlling and manipulative ways.

While Paul lists "fornication" as the outward expression of broken sexuality, his trajectory inward to its source reveals that he is dealing with far more than physical sexuality. Paul roots broken sexuality in "the covetousness, which is idolatry" (v. 5). Covetousness is a primary characteristic of our false self. Our false self covets others, things and the world. We desire to create from these a life of our own choosing, where our desires, our purposes, our agendas are fulfilled and our wants and needs met. In brief, our false self seeks to create a world in which we play God, the ultimate idolatry.

Paul's call for us to put to death the dynamics of our broken sexuality, therefore, probes the heart of our false self. Paul is exhorting us to put to death the idolatry of our false self and its covetousness. Trying to "put to death" the secondary aspects of our broken sexuality—fornication, immorality, lust and evil passion—without abandoning our covetous, idolatrous false self results only in "whitewashed tombs," outwardly beautiful and inwardly full of deadness.

OUR VIOLENCE

What happens when I use my maleness to manipulate you, to control you, to shape our relationship according to my agenda? Unless there is a pathology in you, you are going to resist me. Your resistance may be no more than your false self seeking to out-manipulate me and drawing me into your agenda. Your resistance, whatever its cause, frustrates me. I have this wonderful plan for your life, and you are not letting me program you with it. If you continue to resist my manipulations, my frustration will deepen and become *anger* toward you at the point of your resistance. Continued resistance will move my anger to *wrath,* a more general rage toward you, not just at the point of your resistance. Now other things you do in our relationship begin to feed this wrath until it becomes *malice,* an emotion that desires to harm you in some way. This malice easily becomes *slander,* a denial of your humanity, a demonization of you that will excuse my abusive speech, whatever form in might take. It may be words or it may be actions, but in any case I will react toward you with some form of violence.

Perhaps a prime example in our day is road rage. One person maneuvers their vehicle in such a way that it frustrates the agenda of other drivers, prevents them from driving the way they want, intrudes into their space on the road. An offended driver may lean on the horn, tailgate or try to get ahead of the offender so as to do the same thing to the offender. The other driver then reacts aggressively and a spiral of violence is begun that often results in tragedy.

We see here that the two lists Paul gives us are simply two aspects of a single reality. Broken sexuality and violence form the double helix of our false self, in which its fearful, protective, possessive, manipulative, destructive, self-promoting, indulgent, distinction-making DNA continually replicates itself and infects the world with its cancerous virus.

OUR FALSENESS WITH OTHERS

Finally, Paul exhorts us, "Don't be false with one another" (Col 3:9). Most translations of this passage have something like, "Don't lie to one another," as if it were one more element in the previous list of vices. It is not! The Greek verb Paul uses gives us our English prefix *pseudo,* which has the same meaning in English as in

Greek—"false." Of course, one way we can be false with another person is to lie to them, but Paul is operating at a far deeper level here.

Not only are we created to find our wholeness in a life of loving union with God, but in that union we are to be persons in whom God's love, mercy and grace touch the lives of others. When I use my maleness to manipulate, control or coerce you into my agenda and then further dehumanize and abuse you when you resist me, I am not being the person God created me to be in my relationship with you. I am being false with you.

Suddenly, Paul has rooted our life of loving union with God in the context of our relationships with others. We often think that the place we abandon the vices is in the privacy of our inner self. While there is truth here—the abandonment must be our relinquishment of the self-referenced core of our false self—the place where that abandonment is incarnated is in our relationships with others. Paul points us to the same reality Jesus emphasized in the two symbiotic aspects of the

Great Commandment: "The first is: 'you shall love the Lord your God with all your heart, soul, mind and strength,' and the second is: 'you shall love your neighbor as yourself'" (Mk 12:30-31). When we hear "the first," our false self immediately presumes that loving the Lord our God with all our heart, soul, mind and strength is the all-important thing. So we engage in various types of spiritual practices; we may become rigorously religious; we become very "spiritual" in our efforts to love God with all our heart, soul, mind and strength. We figure once we really get our act together in loving God as we should, perhaps we can then work on loving our neighbor as our self. After all, didn't Jesus say this comes second?

This is not what Jesus is saying. The best translation is: " 'You shall love the Lord, your God, with all your heart, soul, mind and strength.' Another way to say the same thing is, 'You shall love your neighbor as yourself.'" If you think I'm playing fast and loose with Scripture, you haven't read 1 John lately. John got it. He understood that our relationship with God and our relationships with others are two sides of a single coin, the symbiosis of life in loving union with God for others.[3] The place where we live out our relationship of loving union with God is not in the quiet of our prayer closet but in our relationships with one another. Here is where we "put to death" the manipulative, coercive, controlling dynamics of the false self. Here is where we abandon the dehumanizing and abusive practices of the false self. We love others.

Jesus emphasizes this in another way when he teaches us to pray "Our Father in heaven" (Mt 6:9). These four words, prayed with integrity, structure a whole new mode of being in the world. The first word, *our,* indicates that when I initiate openness to God in prayer, I don't do it alone. I come to God within the matrix of all the relationships of my life, actual and potential. I come to God in the context of life in human community, in both the broadest and the narrowest sense. The entire human family is caught up in my "our," as well as the closer web of my daily relationships and the intimate web of my deepest relationships. In the word *our* my relationship with God and my relationships with others are inseparably joined.

When we pray "Our *Father*" with integrity, the context of all our human relationships is transformed. Every person encompassed by *our* becomes our sister and brother. Others are no longer valued for the ways they enhance our agenda or devalued for the ways they thwart our agenda. Others can no longer be pawns in our game, objects for the fulfillment of our desires or enemies to be demonized and destroyed. Every person becomes one whom God loves and for whom God's grace is constantly poured out. We are to be the sister or brother through whom God's love and grace touches the other. "Our Father" instantly bonds us with God on the one hand and with others on the other hand.

When we pray "Our Father *in heaven*" with integrity, all of our life is grounded in a radically alternative mode of being. *In heaven* is not a statement of location, it is the affirmation of God's realm of being in which the "our" can find wholeness of life in loving union with God. *In heaven* affirms a realm whose values, perspectives and practices are contrary to those of our false self; a realm which, as Jesus said, is already in our midst (Lk 17:21).

It becomes unmistakably clear, both from Paul and Jesus (to say nothing of 1 John) that in a profoundly significant way our relationship with God *is* our relationship with others and our relationship with others *is* our relationship with God.

A HUMBLING EXAMPLE

Let me share with you an embarrassing and humbling personal example that illustrates how our relationship with God and with others is inseparably connected. Recently I was traveling on the Metro (train) of a major European city during rush hour. The Metro cars were sardine cans. I was changing trains and waiting for the next train to continue my journey. As I stood on the platform awaiting the next train, I hoped for two things: that the press of the crowd around me wouldn't push me under the train, and that when the train came enough people would get off the car to enable me to squeeze in.

As the train stopped, I was amazed to see that the car which had stopped in front of me was only half full. Actually, it was full but all the people had crowded into the front two-thirds of the car for some reason. The reason became clear the moment I stepped into the empty end of the car. An overpowering stench assailed my nostrils and I discovered that at the empty end of the car was a very dirty and disheveled man sitting on the bench, leaning forward with his head in his hands and a pool of vomit at his feet. I stood for only a moment beside him and then, like the rest, joined the crowd pressed into the front of the car as far from him as possible.

Two nights later I had a dream. It was one of those waking dreams, so real it was almost as if it were actually happening. I was again in that Metro car, standing with the crowd avoiding the derelict. For some reason my attention was focused on the man. As I looked at him, he raised his head, turned and looked directly at me. He was Jesus!

I awoke weeping. My heart wept. I had failed. I heard those terrible words, "I was sick and you did not come to me" (Mt 25:43). My false self, in its fearful, protective distinction making, had not included this man in its "our" Father. I had not allowed that man to be my brother and, in so doing, had denied God as my Father. I had been false with him and with every other person in the car who might have seen something of God's love and grace incarnate had I sat beside that man and comforted him. I am now struggling to pray with integrity "Our Father" as the subtext of all my relationships. This practice in itself has a marvelous way of disclosing those aspects of our false self that must be "put to death."

PUTTING OFF THE OLD NATURE

How then can we avoid being false with others? Paul indicates two things that are required: "Put off the old nature with its practices, and put on the new nature, which is being renewed in knowledge according to the image of its Creator" (Col 3:9-10). There must be a commitment at the core of our being to abandon the entire self-referenced structure of our false self and its embodiment in our relationships. Notice how Paul deals with both our being (the old nature) and our doing (its practices). Our religious false self deals only with our doing, hiding our self-referenced being behind a façade of religious behaviors. As we have seen, it is the covetous idolatry of our false self that must be put to death.

We need to recall the structure Paul has used to describe genuine discipleship. "Put to death" (Col 3:5) is parallel with "Since you died with Christ" (Col 2:20). The entire self-referenced structure of our false self has been revealed as dead in the cross. In a sense we can't put to death our false self. To do so would be just one more self-referenced act that would have to be put to death in order to be restored in loving union with God. In Christ, God has already put the false self to death (2 Cor 5:14). Our role is to acknowledge this reality. I don't mean, however, simply an intellectual assent to a theological fact, a cognitive affirmation of dogma. I mean a proactive acknowledgment of losing our self for Christ's sake, of denying our self, of taking up our cross, of being crucified with Christ: a radical abandonment of our entire self-referenced structure of being. Such abandonment has its roots, in each relationship and situation, in a deep inner release of our false self to God and the daily relinquishment of the manipulative and abusive practices of our false self through which we are false with others.

To put to death your false self is to actualize in your own experience its death in the cross. We do this by the classical discipline of detachment, a central spiritual discipline through the centuries. Peter urges us to "abstain from the desires of the flesh that wage war against the soul" (1 Pet 2:11 NRSV). Paul tells us to "abstain from every form of evil" (1 Thess 5:22 NRSV) and that "those who belong to

Christ Jesus have crucified the flesh with its passions and desires" (Gal 5:24 NRSV). Detachment, however, is more than mere abstinence from certain activities; it is our relinquishment of the deep inner desires that lead to those activities. Such relinquishment, such detachment, however, can become yet another self-generated attempt to achieve holiness—the activity of our religious false self. Detachment, to be genuine, must be a corollary of our loving attachment to God. Detachment is our heartfelt "yes" to Jesus' question, "Do you love me more than these?" (Jn 21:15 NRSV).

Our false self, having removed the roots of our identity, meaning, value and purpose from loving union with God, sinks those roots into multiple alternative soils where we seek to find our identity, meaning, value and purpose. Among such soils are our sexuality, our possessions, our status, our profession, our performances, our relationships, our woundedness, our resentments, our bitterness, our culture, our ethnicity, our place (geographical, emotional, psychological), our intellect, our education, ad infinitum. Our false self has constructed a complex nexus of soils in which the roots of our very being are grounded. Detachment is the discipline of removing our roots from those soils and offering those roots to God. Such detachment is difficult and painful. Detachment is the ongoing process of disconnecting our false self from all our life-support systems (or, in reality, its death-support systems). Our false self will resist such detachment with unbelievable power. We will even become fanatically religious as long as we don't have to lose our self.

Paul points us to such detachment, fatal to our false self, when he exhorts: "I appeal to you therefore, brothers and sisters, by the mercies of God, to present your bodies as a living sacrifice, holy and acceptable to God, which is your spiritual worship" (Rom 12:1 NRSV). The body Paul is speaking of here is that dead body of our false self (our flesh life), which he discusses in Romans 7—8.[4] For our false self to detach the roots of our identity, meaning, value and purpose from the sources of their sustenance is a living sacrifice of profound proportions. It is literally a putting to death. The fatal attraction of our false self to those sources of its nurture requires an equally fatal detachment. We will never experience life in loving union with God as long as the roots of our identity, meaning, value and purpose are grounded in something other than God.

You are probably thinking, *How is such detachment possible?* Am I to give up my home, my family, my job, my network of relationships, my activities, my life? When framed in these terms, detachment begins to sound strangely and disconcertingly familiar: "Whoever comes to me and does not hate father and mother, wife and children, brothers and sisters, yes, and even life itself, cannot be my disciple. Whoever does not carry the cross and follow me cannot be my disciple" (Lk 14:26-27 NRSV). This word of Jesus has been horribly abused by religious false selves who have used it as an excuse for abandoning all responsibilities for family. But what does Jesus mean? I don't believe detachment means the abandonment of most of the relationships, structures and activities of our lives. It means, in those very relationships, structures and activities, *to do for Jesus' sake what formerly we did for our own.* [5] Such a radical reorientation is, at one and the same time, both the putting to death of our false self and the putting on of our new nature hidden with Christ in God.

How might we begin the discipline of detachment? Here is a simple exercise that can have profound effects in your life. In many of his introductions to his letters Paul writes, "Paul, an apostle of Jesus Christ through the will of God."[6] Take out Paul's name and insert yours. Take out *apostle* and insert the various roles you fulfill in your life—husband or wife, mother or father, son or daughter, employer or employee and so on. Now read the sentence. This should radically reframe every role you fulfill in your life because it reminds you that the true fulfillment of each role is a life hidden with Christ in God and a role in which you are to be God's person. You might consider writing that sentence on a slip of paper or small card for each role you fulfill and placing it in a prominent place in the space where you regularly fulfill that role. Each time you find yourself returning to your self-referenced way of living in that role, detach yourself by inwardly (or even verbally) saying, "Lord, help me to love you more than this," and then enter back into that role with Christ at the center rather than you, with God's purposes foremost rather than yours, desiring for Christ to be manifest in you.

PUTTING ON THE NEW NATURE

Putting to death the false self, therefore, is not only a matter of negation. It is more a matter of confirmation: "put on the new nature, which is being renewed in knowledge according to the image of its Creator" (Col 3:10). In a sense Paul is reemphasizing what he said in Colossians 3:3: "You have died, and your life is hidden with Christ in God" (NRSV). Putting on the new nature, as with putting off the old, is not something we can do. This too would be an act of self-referenced effort, which would be the antithesis of our new nature's loving abandonment to God. Paul immediately follows, therefore, with, "which is *being renewed*." The growth and development of our new nature is God's doing, not ours. Just as putting off our old nature is a matter of acknowledging its deadness and abandoning it, detaching it from the roots of its nurture, so putting on the new nature is a matter of acknowledging our life hidden with Christ in God as the reality of our being, sending the roots of our being deeply into God's love, and incarnating it in our lives with others. Paul will unpack what this looks like for us in the last section (Col 3:12-17).

Such acknowledgment is far more than our intellectual assent to a theological fact or our cognitive affirmation of dogma. It is a radical commitment to a whole new mode of being. It is "striving for the things above," the act of "orienting our whole being to the things above" (Col 3:1-2). It is sending the roots of our being deep into the soil of God's love. Paul indicates that our new nature "is being renewed in knowledge according to the image of its Creator." The word Paul uses for knowledge indicates experiential knowledge, not merely cognitive knowledge. As we commit ourselves unreservedly to the life hidden with Christ in God, through the regenerating work of the Holy Spirit within us, we begin to experience the life of Christ within us as our own life. As Paul says of his own experience, "it is no longer I who live, but it is Christ who lives in me" (Gal 2:20 NRSV). The root of our new nature is a radical abandonment to God in love in the depths of our heart, and the fruit is a radical availability to God for others. Thomas Merton describes it as "a disposition of our whole being, brought about by that Love which so likens and conforms us to God that we become able to experience Him mystically in and through our inmost selves, as if He were our very selves."[7]

The focus of putting on our new nature, as with putting off our old, is in our relationships with others. Paul tells us that in our new nature "there is neither Greek nor Jew, circumcised or uncircumcised, barbarian or Scythian, slave or free; but Christ is all and in all" (Col 3:11). These are the kinds of distinctions our false self creates to protect and promote our self with respect to others: racial (Greek-Jew), religious (circumcised-uncircumcised), cultural (barbarian-Scythian), social-economic (slave-free), and we could add age, gender, ethnic, political and so forth. Such distinctions simply have no function in our life hidden with Christ in God. When we pray "Our Father" with integrity, all these secondary human distinctions fall away, and others become those for whom we are brother or sister, those to whom God reaches out in love, mercy and grace.

Paul closes his portrayal of our new nature with the mysterious claim, "Christ is all and in all." What does he mean? It seems when Paul says "Christ is all," he is indicating that for our life hidden with Christ in God, Christ becomes the sole defining reality. As he says to the Philippians, "For to me, living is Christ" (Phil 1:21 NRSV).

Thomas Merton put it like this: "The [person] who lives and acts according to the grace of Christ dwelling in [him or her], acts in that case as another Christ, as a son [or daughter] of God, and thus ... prolongs in [his or her] own life the effects and the miracle of the incarnation."[8] Mystical, yes, but exactly what we have seen Jesus pray for us: "That they may all be one. As you, Father, are in me and I am in you, may they also be in us, so that the world may believe that you have sent me" (Jn 17:21 NRSV). Jesus prays that we may be in the same relationship with God as he is as the revelation of our true humanness so that in the world we may be the manifestation of his presence. Both in our being, and in our doing, Christ is all.

The other half of Paul's statement is that "Christ is ... in all." The deep truth of this aspect of the life hidden with Christ in God was beautifully illustrated by Mother Teresa of Calcutta. When Mother Teresa took a dying derelict from the gutters of Calcutta, the most marginalized of the marginalized, she knew she was taking

Christ from that gutter. When she washed the filth from that emaciated body, she knew she was washing the body of Christ. When she anointed the festering sores of that person, she knew she was bringing healing to Christ. When she fed that starving person, she knew she was feeding Christ. And when she held that dying person in her arms and gave him or her love and comfort in the last moments, she knew she was holding Christ. For Mother Teresa, Christ was in all. To be sure, she spoke of this as Christ in his distressing disguise, but nonetheless Christ! If Mother Teresa had entered that Metro car with me, she would have seen Christ in the derelict sitting in his vomit. You see, Mother Teresa was putting off the old nature and its practices and was putting on the new nature that was being renewed in knowledge according to the image of its Creator, where "Christ is all and in all."

You might say, "Well, that was Mother Teresa, and I am no Mother Teresa." I am sure she would say to you, "Why not? Doesn't Christ meet you every day in his distressing disguises?

Is he not present in those persons who impinge upon your life in unexpected and uncomfortable ways? Is he not beside you in the office as the unnoticed and underappreciated person who takes care of menial chores? Is he not there in that street person you pass every day without acknowledging him or her? Is he not in your spouse? In your children? In your neighbor?"

CONCLUSION

Well, what do you make of all this?

- Where has God been probing aspects of your false self, especially your religious false self, with the call to put to death that false self?
- Are there serious changes you need to make in your understanding of your false self?
- Have you seen something of the deadness of your false self that you need to abandon?
- How about your relationships with others? Where do you see the fruits of the false self poisoning those relationships? Can you identify some

of the ways in which you are "false with others"?

Perhaps you might begin to make "Our Father" the undercurrent of all your relationships.

Perhaps you might begin to view the "uncomfortable" people in your life as Christ in his "disturbing disguise."

But above all, I invite you to seek to abandon yourself to God in love and become radically available to God for others.

6

PUTTING ON THE NEW NATURE

Loving God, something deep within me hungers for wholeness. Voiceless stirrings in the depths of my being surprise me at unexpected moments with their intimation of a life in you, which would transfigure me and transform my life in this world. These all-too-brief moments of clarity, these glimpses of a richer life, quickly fade beneath the constant onslaught of my daily life, its pressures, its problems, its pernicious inertia. Yet your presence continues to reside in my depths, your love calls forth those hungers for wholeness; your grace engenders those voiceless stirrings. As I look now at Paul's invitation to put on this new nature, may your Spirit anoint what I read and think so as to give voice to these voiceless stirrings. Enable me to not *only hear your voice but respond to your love from the depths of my being. Amen.*

One of the greatest detriments to a growing and maturing life in loving union with God is focusing too much on avoiding the vices, on putting to death our false self. Even if we could rid the soil of our life of every weed, every evil growth, all that would remain is a barren, sterile plot of dust. Our vices must be replaced with virtues; our false self supplanted by our life hidden with Christ in God. This is why Paul, as he concludes his section on putting to death our false self, inseparably conjoins "having put off the old nature with its deeds" with "having put on the new nature which is being renewed" (Col 3:9-10).

GOD' S CHOSEN ONES

Paul introduces his section on putting on the new nature (Col 3:12-17) with a rather strange affirmation. He addresses his readers as "God's chosen ones, holy and beloved" (v. 12 NRSV). This affirmation comes as a surprise after what Paul has inferred about his readers. They have been portrayed as the epitome of religious false selves, people who need a radical reorientation of their entire beings and a realization of their true nature in Christ. Paul's readers obviously still operate out of the manipulative and abusive dynamics of the false self, otherwise he would not have exhorted them to put these to death and stop being false with each other. How is it, then, that he addresses them (and us) as "God's chosen ones, holy and beloved"?

Well, our identification as God's chosen ones actually has nothing to do with us. This is an affirmation of God's unfathomably loving purpose for us. As we saw in chapter four, we are spoken forth out of the heart of God's love from before the foundation of the world (Eph 1:4). Our nature as "God's chosen [spoken forth][1] ones" is not something that comes to us after the fact of our existence. It is not that somewhere along the trajectory of our life God one day decided to choose us and began to love us. Our chosenness is the profound reality out of which our very being has emerged. We were chosen to be in the heart of God long before we ever existed in this life. Henri Nouwen puts it well:

> The spiritual life starts at the place where you can hear God's voice. Where somehow you can claim that long before your father, your mother, your brother, your sister, your school, your church touched you, loved you, and wounded you—long before that, you were held safe in an eternal embrace. You were seen with eyes of perfect love long before you entered into the dark valley of life.... The spiritual life starts at the moment that you can go beyond all of the wounds and claim that there was a love that was perfect and unlimited, long before that perfect love became reflected in the imperfect and limited, conditional love of people. The spiritual life starts where you dare to claim the first love.[2]

Nouwen illustrates not only what it means to be God's chosen ones but also to be beloved. Our state of chosenness is not some arbitrary, authoritarian matrix in which we are imprisoned like birds in a cage. We are chosen in love and for love. We are spoken forth out of the heart of God's love so that we might not only know that love but find our perfect wholeness in loving union with God. Being beloved is no more our doing than being God's chosen ones. The unfathomable depths of our belovedness is revealed in the cruciform love of God in Christ. When we turn away from God's love and become selfreferenced beings, false selves, God's love continues to enfold us and indwell us, now as a cruciform love at the heart of our false self. Even when we are most alienated from God by our self-referenced life, we are still beloved. This is why the mothers and fathers of our spiritual tradition have consistently insisted that there is nothing we can do to make God love us more. "God substantiates his own love for us in that while we were still sinners, Christ died for us" (Rom 5:8).

Even if our "chosenness" and "belovedness" are God's doing, not ours, how can Paul call the Colossians (and us) "holy"? I don't think it is by accident that Paul places *holy* between *chosen* and *beloved.* These three terms also appear together in Ephesians 1:4, where Paul says we were spoken forth (chosen) before the foundation of the world that we might be holy and blameless before God in love. Holiness is not some regimen of abstinence or a life of rigorous religiosity; holiness is life in the image of God: "You shall be holy, for I the LORD your God am holy" (Lev 19:2 NRSV). Holiness is life in loving union with God. Such a life is our wholeness, our maturity, our fullness, that for which we were created. Just as an acorn finds its fulfillment and maturity in a mighty oak tree, so we find our ultimate fulfillment and complete maturity in being holy. Holiness is not some alien form of life imposed on us from without. It is the flowering of the very nature of our true being from within. It is the nature of our true being because of our chosenness; it flowers into maturity out of our belovedness. The cruciform love of God, which plumbs the depths of our unholiness, is, at the same time, the sanctifying love of God that raises us to life in loving union with God and nurtures us to wholeness (holiness) in that loving union.

With his affirmation that we are "God's chosen ones, holy and beloved," Paul provides us with the foundation (chosen), the purpose (holy) and the means (beloved) of our true life, the life hidden with Christ in God. Paul may preface his exhortations for us to put on the new nature with this affirmation because he is fully aware of the difficulty of what is to follow. To put on the new nature is the ultimate death blow to the false self.

PUTTING ON THE VIRTUES

Put on, then, Paul says, "compassion, kindness, lowliness, gentleness, patience" (Col 3:12). Once again Paul makes the inseparable connection between our life with God and our life with others. We can put on none of these virtues in a privatized, individualized relationship with God. Each of them is situated in the midst of our often messy relationships with others. We can't be compassionate in the quiet of our prayer closet but only in the often difficult and unpleasant noise of our relationship with another person. We can't be kind all by ourselves but only in a relationship, and particularly when we are tempted to be unkind or mean rather than to be kind. We can't be lowly in the privacy of our room but only in relationships with others, and especially in those relationships where our impulse is to exalt ourselves over others. We can't be humble with ourselves but only in our life with others, particularly where our pride tends to surface. We can't be patient by ourselves but only in relationships with others and predominantly in those where impatience is the norm.

I hope you can see that putting on the virtues of our new nature takes place in the midst of our everyday life with others. Can you also see that these disciplines strike a death blow at our false self and its self-referenced structure of relationships with others? Genuine *compassion* requires a loving immersion in the life of others, a feeling of their pain, a sharing of their hurt, being touched deep in our own being by their brokenness. Such immersion is costly, in time, energy, attentiveness and perhaps even material resources. Our false self, if we get involved at all, quickly applies a bandage and moves on. Losing our self for another in this way is not part of our false self's agenda. Others are to be either benefactors or servants of our false self, not the other way around.

Kindness that is more than condescension calls for a sincere consideration for another person, a sensitivity to their tenderness and their weakness. More than this, kindness requires seeing others as persons of value and worth in and of themselves. It calls us to respect their integrity and not act in a way that might cause them to be shamed, disadvantaged or marginalized. Kindness is seen as weakness by our false self. To be kind is to make our self vulnerable to the possible intrigues and manipulations of others. To deny our self control over another by being kind is anathema for our false self.

The *lowliness* that considers others of inestimable value, no matter what their status or station in life, the lowliness that stoops beneath them to raise them up, the lowliness that acknowledges they may be way ahead of us in areas that we thought ourselves to be superior in—such lowliness is unknown and totally unrealistic to our false self. Lowliness is the unquestioned position of others, not of our false self, even though we may at times masquerade behind a false lowliness to gain some benefit for our self. Our false self would die before we would become truly lowly. Of course, that is exactly what we must do to be so.

True *gentleness,* or meekness, comes from a radical abandonment to God in love that frees us from the defensive, protective, self-promoting structures of our false self. If there is any gentleness in our false self it is usually the velvet glove masking the iron fist. To be gentle when another is harsh, to be meek when another is overbearing is, for our false self, to be abysmally weak and to endanger our control, position and power. In reality, genuine gentleness introduces the presence of unlimited grace into the relationship.

Patience, or longsuffering, is the virtue that attacks the root of our false self's need to advance its own agenda. When others stand in the way of the fulfillment of our plans and purposes, especially when we are convinced these are God's plans and purposes, our false self is anything but patient. Frustration, anger, outrage and coercion are merely some of the consequences of our impatience. Patience is not a tense waiting for the others to come around to our agenda but a willingness to allow God to work in God's way and in God's time to bring everyone, ourselves included, to God's agenda for the situation.

You can see that these virtues of a life hidden with Christ in God strike at the very core of our false self. They do this in the midst of our daily life in relationships with others. It is here, in the midst of these relationships, that we are to put on the new nature. This is another aspect of the reality that our life with God and our life with others are two sides of an indivisible whole. In the midst of our relationships we are to put to death the dehumanizing manipulation and destructive violence of our false self by putting on the virtues of a life hidden with Christ in God.

If you have difficulties with these aspects of the new nature, is it because they are rubbing against the grain of your false self? Perhaps you realize that to relate to others as Paul enjoins us would radically change the nature of all your relationships, from the closest to the most tangential, and such changes would call into question your very identity, value, meaning and purpose as you understand them. You may have the gnawing awareness that the whole façade of your false self, especially your religious false self, might implode if you began to live by these virtues, and it scares you to death. You may realize that to put on this new nature would require you to abandon your comfortable life as usual.

It may already be dawning on you that each day God places before us multiple opportunities to put on the new nature in each relationship of that day. Numerous times every day we have situations in relationships with others where we could put on compassion or kindness or lowliness or gentleness or patience or any combination of these. Doing so cuts the roots of our false self in our self-referenced pride, protectiveness, defensiveness, manipulation and abusiveness, and provides God with an opportunity to nurture in us the life hidden with Christ.

HOW TO PUT ON THE VIRTUES

But how do we do this? Paul provides us two basic contexts in which we are to put on the virtues: relationships in which we must (1) *forbear one another,* and (2) *forgive one another* (Col 3:13). Many translations make these appear as if they are two more items on the list of virtues. Paul's Greek is unmistakably clear, however. Forbearing and forgiving are not two more items on the list. They are the contexts in which we put on the virtues of the new nature.[3]

Forbearing one another. What does it mean for us to be forbearing with another? Perhaps the best understanding of forbearing is letting others be who they are. Our false self rarely relates to others as they are. Our false self relates to others from what we perceive them to be from our own self-referenced perspective. Not only does our false self contain God in a box of our own making, it contains others in boxes as well. The boxes in which we try to imprison others are designed to assure that the other will be what we want them to be in our carefully constructed world. It keeps them at arm's length. It keeps them relatively safe. The box by which we control others enables us to accommodate them to our agendas. It also provides us some level of protection and defense against the threat they pose to our control of the world. Such boxes also blind us to who the other truly is. They become a caricature, largely of our own creation, with whom we relate from within our self-referenced frames of reference. Strangers pose a real threat to our false self because they have not yet been boxed in order to determine how we should relate to them (or whether we should relate to them at all). People who don't stay in their box are an even greater problem for our false self. They become loose cannons who threaten the fragile stability we have constructed in our relationship with them. More than this, they threaten our own construct of who we perceive ourselves to be; they rattle the walls of our own box.

Our religious false self adds yet another veneer to the box in which we impound others. Our religious false self tends to relate to others from within our own perspective of what it means to be religious. Others are judged and their box constructed in light of our evaluation of their religiosity. Their weaknesses, flaws and imperfections all become sins, which paint their box in dark colors. Our religious false self then either avoids or severely limits relationships with such persons, or begins a crusade to remake them in our own model of religiosity.

To be forbearing with others requires the relinquishment of the boxes in which we imprison them. It also calls for the abandonment of the box that we have constructed as the matrix of our false self's identity, value, meaning and purpose. To be forbearing is to entrust ourselves to God in love to such an extent that we can be available to God for the other, willing to be one in whom God can be present for the other in whatever way God chooses. We can never be one in whom God is present for others unless we come to them as they are in their own being. This does not mean to confirm others in their sin, woundedness, brokenness, darkness or deadness. If, however, God is ever to be present in us for their cleansing, their healing, their wholeness, their enlightenment, their resurrection to transformed life, we must enter into relationship with them as they are.

Christ is the model of such forbearance. In the letter to Laodicea Jesus says, "I stand at the door and knock. If anyone hears my voice and opens the door I will come in to them and eat with them and they with me" (Rev 3:20). Jesus meets us at the door of our false self, at that place in our life where we have shut him out and are imprisoned by our self-referenced structure of being. Note again that Jesus does not say we are to come out to him. He says he will come in to us. He will meet us in the midst of our false self and nurture us to wholeness there. In forbearance he meets us where we are.

To forbear others is to come to them in the bondage of their false self and to be for them one in whom God's love knocks on the closed doors of their life with compassion, kindness, lowliness, gentleness, patience.

Isn't forbearance, then, simply a sanitized way of being a doormat for others? Not at all. To relate to others as they are does not mean allowing them to be destructive toward us. Forbearance, however, does not resist their destructive behaviors with the defensive and protective postures of our false self, which simply inflicts our destructiveness on others. The resistance to their destructive behaviors is itself the manifestation of compassion, kindness, lowliness, gentleness and patience. Our life hidden with Christ in

God is not engaged in defending itself against the destructive behaviors of the other but always seeks the welfare and wholeness of the other. Now it may be that in restraining the destructive behaviors of another, we experience in our own being their destructive actions. This then is where we enter into the experience of cruciform love.

Forgiving one another. At this point Paul brings us to the second and most difficult context in which we put on the virtues: "*forgive one another if anyone has a complaint against another*" (Col 3:13). It appears that Paul has overlooked an essential detail here. He says nothing about others crawling to us on their knees to beg our forgiveness. After all, how can we forgive a person who does not acknowledge the wrong they have done to us? Paul answers, "Unconditionally!"

Here our false self rises up in righteous indignation. For our false self, forgiveness is an act of gracious superiority bestowed when the one who has wronged us cringes before us in abject humility. Such forgiveness is an act that elevates our false self over the one who wronged us and provides a point of leverage we can use to manipulate the other in the future. Our false self requires "justice" (spelled r-e-v-e-n-g-e) before forgiveness can be granted. The offender must be repentant, apologetic (often publicly), provide restitution for loss or injury, perhaps even make a commitment not to repeat the behavior; then, *perhaps* our false self might consider forgiveness.

We see here a complete misunderstanding of the nature of forgiveness. We assume forgiveness is something we do for the one who wronged us. This is not the forgiveness Paul calls us to. The forgiveness Paul urges here is an act that, by God's grace, releases us from the destructive bondage of what the other did to us. When we have been wronged by another, that wrong becomes a festering sore, a developing cancer in our soul, that not only degrades our relationship with the one who wronged us but also degrades all other relationships. Having been deeply wounded in one relationship, we become hypersensitive and defensive in all other relationships to insure that we are not hurt in that way again. The resentment and bitterness we nurture in our spirit against the one who abused us becomes a poison that pervades all other relationships. Our life has been taken captive by the one who wronged us, and as we dwell in the recurring memory of what they did to us, the walls of our prison become thicker and thicker.

If we will not forgive unconditionally, as Paul exhorts us, what will we do regarding the one who has terribly abused us and has died? They will never come crawling to us begging our forgiveness. What will we do about the person who doesn't even acknowledge the wrong done? He or she may never seek our forgiveness.

The forgiveness Paul calls us to is a radical act. Lance Morrow reviewed Pumla Gobodo-Madikizela's book, *A Human Being Died That Night: A South African Story of Forgiveness,* which is a psychologist's study of Eugene de Kock, the commander of the state-sanctioned apartheid death squads. Morrow reports, "Gobodo-Madikizela knows that forgiveness is less a matter of understanding than of a more profound motion of the heart—a transcendence. *The importance is not so much that it absolves the one forgiven as that it cleanses the one who forgives."* [4]

We should quickly note that the forgiveness Paul enjoins is not a special formula for reconciliation. If we forgive in this unconditional way, it does not mean that the one who wronged us will repent, apologize, make restitution and restore the relationship. Reconciliation is an entirely different matter. It must also be noted, however, that this unconditional forgiveness is the only sound preparation for reconciliation from our side. Without such forgiveness, should the one who wronged us come in repentance and apologize, our response will be more engendered by our need for "justice" than our readiness to forgive.

Paul is not the only one who calls us to such unconditional forgiveness. In the Lord's Prayer Jesus teaches us to pray, "Forgive us our sins as we forgive those who sin against us" (Mt 6:12).

Again, there is no mention of the person who wronged us repenting, apologizing, making restitution and begging our forgiveness. Here Jesus links our unconditional forgiveness to our relationship with God. This is the only portion of the prayer that Jesus amplifies further: "For if you forgive others their sins, your heavenly Father will forgive you; but if you do not forgive others, your heavenly Father will not forgive your sins" (Mt 6:14-15). We tend to read this as if God were petulant, as if God says, "Well, if you won't forgive them, I won't forgive you." What Jesus is stating in a radical way is that our unforgiveness profoundly affects our relationship with God. Not only does our unforgiveness lock us into the bondage of what the other did to us, it shuts us off from God as well. Our bitterness, our resentment, our desire for revenge and our unforgiveness choke off our openness to God, clog our receptors of God's grace and render us incapable of receiving God's forgiveness. Unforgiveness fuels the self-referenced dynamics of our false self, which close us to God.

To say that unconditional forgiveness is difficult is an understatement of colossal proportions. Let me share with you a personal experience. Several years ago a person who was very close to me, someone I'll call Chris, came to me at the close of a very difficult situation. As far as Chris was concerned I no longer existed. Chris no longer wanted anything to do with me, didn't want to hear from me, didn't want to see me. Having delivered this ultimatum, Chris turned and walked away, without allowing time for questions, response or retort. I was devastated! While we had just been through a difficult situation, I had not picked up any signals indicating such a profound level of pain and hurt on Chris's part.

For about a month I was in deep shock and grief. I awoke each morning with the physical feeling of a great, heavy weight pressing upon my chest. It felt as if there were a huge ball of lead residing in my chest. I carried this weight through each day and lay down to try to sleep with it at night. During wakeful hours of the night I wrestled with this agonizing burden.

Then, gradually, the burden began to turn poisonous. I began to try to fix blame on Chris, playing the scenario over and over in ways that always put Chris in the wrong. I began to imagine barbed retorts I could have made and those malevolent responses I would make if ever the chance arose. I began to slide down that dangerous slope of bitterness and resentment.

As that slide commenced, however, I began to sense, in my relationship with God, a stirring within awakening me to the destructiveness of the downward path I was sliding on. I became convinced in my heart that I shouldn't go down that path and at the same time began to get a first intimation of this unconditional forgiveness Jesus and Paul call us to. The first stages of transition from bitterness to forgiveness were tortuous. Whenever I caught myself wallowing in resentment and constructing scenarios of revenge, I had to make an effort to turn to God and seek strength to turn away from this course. For months the outcome of the struggle was in doubt. At first I reveled in dreams of revenge far more than I sought God, but gradually God enabled me to turn more and more consistently to God as the bitterness tapes began to replay themselves.

I came to realize that a spiritual discipline to engender unconditional forgiveness would allow me to continue to maintain my relationship with Chris. So I resumed sending birthday cards and presents, Christmas cards and presents, all of which may have gone into a black hole. There was no response, either positive or negative.

It was years before I began to sense in my heart that God had enabled me to forgive. While the pain of the estrangement continued, it seemed to be a clean pain, free of the infection of bitterness and resentment and desire for revenge.

Several years later there was a death in Chris's family, and I was asked to perform the funeral service. While I knew that the person who had died was a very significant person in Chris's life, it didn't occur to me that Chris would be present for the funeral. When I exited from the Jetway into the airport concourse of the city where the funeral was to be held, there, with the person who had come to meet me, was Chris, for whom I didn't exist, along with two others. I thought to myself, *This should be interesting!*

As I approached the group, Chris turned away from me. I greeted the others and, after retrieving my luggage, we went to the car. As it turned out, the only seating arrangement that worked was for Chris and me to sit in the front seat beside the driver. During the entire two-hour journey to the home of the deceased, it was patently obvious that for Chris I wasn't there. Whenever Chris spoke to the group, body language and content of the conversation indicated my nonexistence. We spent the evening at the home of the deceased, and the pattern prevailed. Whenever I contributed to the conversation, Chris made it clear by body language that no one was speaking, and when Chris contributed it was equally obvious there was no one sitting in my chair.

The funeral was held at a funeral home with a large chapel. It was arranged that when the service was over, the family and close friends of the deceased would file out of their seats in the front pews, I would come down from the altar area and fall in behind them, and we would proceed to the reception area to greet those who had come. As the family and close friends were filing out, and I was coming down from the altar area, Chris became lost in grief. Leaning on the screen in front of the first row of pews, Chris sobbed with body-shaking sobs. I was in a quandary. Having officiated at many funerals and experienced many strange things that occur in those settings, I knew what might be done, but what do you do for a person who doesn't acknowledge your existence? Should I leave Chris in grief and follow the family out? Should I go to Chris?

I decided that I should go to Chris. I simply stood in front of Chris and held out my arms in an offer of comfort and support. To my utter surprise and amazement, Chris fell into my arms and cried on my shoulder. Thus the process of restoration began.

Reflecting on this, I came to realize that had God not graciously enabled me to forgive Chris, I would have acted in a far different manner. I would have walked past Chris to follow the family out, gloating in my heart that Chris was "getting it" for the pain and grief I had experienced.

In the years since then, I have come to realize that unforgiveness is a primary issue in the spiritual journey. It is a primary trait of our false self. Any mistreatment, real or imagined, is received by our false self as a blow to our identity, value, meaning and purpose. Everything within rises up in retaliation against the perpetrator of this affront. Our religious false self can be even more terrible in its unforgiveness since we tend to see ill treatment as an attack on our "God" and, consequently, our retaliation is justified on religious grounds.

Conversely, unconditional forgiveness is the cutting edge of a life hidden with Christ in God and, at the same time, a mortal blow to the dominance of our false self. In order to forgive unconditionally the one who has wronged us, our false self must be relinquished. Our anger, resentment, bitterness and push for retaliation, our demand for "justice," all must be relinquished in a radical abandonment to Christ in the midst of our injury and replaced by a consecration to allow Christ to be formed in us through forgiveness.

Such unconditional forgiveness is, from a human standpoint, impossible. Corrie ten Boom shares an experience that powerfully illustrates this truth. Corrie and her family had been sent to the Nazi concentration camps because of their assistance to the Jewish people. After the war, God sent Corrie to tell the German people of God's love and forgiveness. She had spoken to a group of people in a church in Munich and was greeting people as they left when she saw coming toward her one of the cruelest of the guards from Ravensbrück, where she and her sister, Betsy, had been imprisoned.

Corrie writes, "Now he was in front of me, hand thrust out: 'A fine message, Fraulein! How good it is to know that, as you say, all our sins are at the bottom of the sea!'" She said, "My blood seemed to freeze." She remembered vividly her experience and the death of her sister, Betsy. The former guard told Corrie that he had become a Christian since the war and that, while God had forgiven him for his cruelty, he wanted her to forgive him.

Corrie writes, "And I stood there—I whose sins had again and again to be forgiven—and I could not forgive. Betsy had died in that place—could he erase her slow terrible death simply for the asking?" She found herself incapable of feeling forgiveness for this man.

Listen to Corrie's experience:

It could not have been many seconds that he stood there—hand held out—but to me it seemed hours as I wrestled with the most difficult thing I had ever had to do....

And still I stood there with the coldness clutching my heart....

"Jesus, help me!" I prayed silently. "I can lift my hand. I can do that much. You supply the feeling."

And so woodenly, mechanically, I thrust my hand into the one stretched out to me. And as I did, an incredible thing took place. The current started in my shoulder, raced down my arm, sprang into our joined hands. And then this healing warmth seemed to flood my whole being, bringing tears to my eyes.

"I forgive you, brother!" I cried. "With all my heart."

For a long moment we grasped each other's hands, the former guard and the former prisoner. I had never known God's love so intensely as I did then.[5]

PUTTING ON CHRIST

Paul must have known something of this reality of unconditional forgiveness when he added to his exhortation "In addition to all these, put on the love, which is the bond of wholeness" (Col 3:14), a seemingly innocuous phrase.

Its depths, however, are revealed in the Greek text. (I hope you are up for another little Greek lesson.) First, Paul uses the definite article *the,* which, when present in Greek, points to a very specific thing. Paul doesn't say, "Put on love"; he says, "Put on *the* love." This is a very particular love Paul is introducing. Second, Paul commits an unusual grammatical error. In Greek, *love* is a feminine gender noun. However, the relative pronoun Paul uses for *which,* which should be feminine to agree with *love,* is neuter gender. This is a kindergarten type of error, and Paul is very adept in his use of Greek. What's going on?

In Greek, if you want to refer to things of two different genders by using a relative pronoun, you use the neuter for the relative pronoun. Well, we have a feminine gender noun in the word *love,* a neuter relative pronoun in *which,* but where is the third element, in either the masculine or neuter gender, which, when coupled with *love* calls forth the neuter relative pronoun? I would suggest that the missing element is *Christ.* Christ is the love that enables unconditional forgiveness. Paul is indicating that we must "put on Christ" if we are to forgive with compassion, kindness, lowliness, gentleness and patience. In fact, the image is found in Romans 13:14: "Put on the Lord Jesus Christ and take no care for the desires of the flesh."[6] "The flesh" is Paul's term for our false self. The desires of the flesh are anger, resentment, bitterness and retaliation when we have been abused by someone. For us to put on Christ, or to put on the *love* that is the bond of wholeness, is to let our life hidden with Christ in God meet the injury with unconditional forgiveness.

This understanding—that the love we are to put on is Christ—is confirmed in Paul's next two injunctions: "Let the peace of Christ rule in your hearts.... Let the word of Christ dwell in you richly" (Col 3:15-16 NRSV). How can the peace of Christ rule in our hearts, how can the word of Christ dwell in us richly, unless Christ is present in our life? Not present in some theoretical or theological construct but present as an experiential reality, as a living presence, as our true self. Thomas Merton indicates this in a reflection on Ephesians 3:16-19:

It is a question of the inward man springing to life at the spiritual contact of God, in faith. This contact brings one face to face with a reality that is "unseen" first of all, and yet paradoxically, this "seeing" of the "unseen" brings about an ever deepening renewal of life which is "according to knowledge," that is to say according to a genuine experience of Christ, caused by our likeness, or "sonship," by the gift of the divine Spirit Who makes Christ "dwell in our hearts" or in our inmost selves. The result of this indwelling of Christ and of the Holy Spirit is the overflowing fullness of new life, of charity, divine love, and a spiritual comprehension of the mystery of God's life within us in all its dimensions, through the experience of Christ's love for us "which surpasses all understanding."[7]

Paul is making it unmistakably clear that putting on the new nature, which manifests itself in compassion, kindness, lowliness, gentleness and patience as it relates to others with forbearance and unconditional forgiveness, is not merely the adoption of a new set of behaviors and the development of a new mode of relating to others. Putting on the new nature is allowing the real presence of Christ to take control and dominate us, not as a hostile takeover but as a loving union of our being with God in Christ. This reality is what Paul is pointing us to when he says "For me, to live is Christ" (Phil 1:21) and "it is no longer I who live but Christ who lives in me" (Gal 2:20), as well as what he previously indicated to the Colossians, "Your life is hidden with Christ in God," and "Christ, your life" (Col 3:3-4).

The virtues of compassion, kindness, lowliness, meekness and patience, exercised in relationships of forbearance and forgiveness, are merely disparate actions of our religious false self unless they are manifestations of the incarnation of Christ in us. The "bond of wholeness" (v. 14) Paul speaks of here is our union with Christ in God, or to use Paul's earlier image, our life hidden with Christ in God. Ultimately, the virtues flow from loving union with God, the fruits of a life abandoned to God in love. It is only out of such wholeness that our lives become fully actualized as those in whom God dwells for others. Paul makes this clear in what follows.

The peace of Christ is God's shalom, usually thought of as a realm of being in which we and others find wholeness in mutual loving relationship with God. Deeper than this, however, the peace of Christ is the vital and creative union of God and Christ into which we have been invited. Jesus told his disciples, "Peace I leave with you; my peace I give to you" (Jn 14:27 NRSV). To allow the peace of Christ to rule in our hearts we must be as totally abandoned to God in love as Christ is. It is to allow ourselves to be drawn into that oneness with God and Christ for which Jesus prayed: "That they may all be one. As you, Father, are in me and I am in you, may they also be in us.... I in them and you in me, that they may become completely one" (Jn 17:21, 23 NRSV).

Paul makes it clear, however, that this deep union of love with God in Christ is not a privatized, individual experience we can possess for ourselves. Although we are indeed called into this loving union with God, its context is the *one body*. We are not merely called into loving union with God in Christ but into loving union with our sisters and brothers. In our human relationships our relationship with God is lived out, and in our relationship with God our human relationships are lived out. As John so bluntly puts it, "Those who say, 'I love God,' and hate their brothers or sisters, are liars; for those who do not love a brother or sister whom they have seen, cannot love God whom they have not seen" (1 Jn 4:20 NRSV). Only in our relationships with others can the fruits of compassion, kindness, lowliness, meekness and patience—which blossom from our loving union with God in Christ—grow and nurture others.

Paul's next exhortation related to putting on the new nature is a puzzle. "Let the word of Christ dwell in you richly" (Col 3:16 NRSV). This is the only place in all his writings where Paul uses the phrase "the word of Christ."[8] We may get an idea of Paul's meaning from Colossians 4:3, where Paul urges the Colossians to pray for him "that God might open for us a door for the word *[logos]* that we may speak the mystery of Christ." It seems clear in this context that the "word" is "the mystery of Christ." Paul has earlier indicated to the Colossians his desire that they have "the knowledge of God's mystery, that is, Christ himself" (Col 2:2 NRSV).[9] He had previously clarified this mystery as "Christ in you, the hope of glory" (Col 1:27 NRSV).[10] When Paul exhorts us to "let the word of Christ dwell in you richly," he seems to be indicating that we are to be thoroughly Christ-referenced. The very presence of Christ indwelling us in the depths of our being is to be the primal reality of our life.

This reality of Christ indwelling us and shaping our life is not a privatized, individualized experience. It forms the context of our relationships with others—"as you teach and instruct one another in all wisdom," and with

God—"as you sing songs and hymns and spiritual songs to God in your heart with thankfulness" (v. 16). Paul had previously told the Colossians how he had "taught and instructed everyone in all wisdom in order to present every person mature in Christ" (Col 1:28). Surely this contextualizes our teaching and instructing "one another in all wisdom." Such activity is a mutual nurturing of one another toward maturity in Christ, a radical abandonment of our self to Christ in love, and our radical availability to Christ for others in which we become one in whom Christ dwells for the nurture of others and others are likewise indwelt by Christ for our nurture. Paul here seems to be amplifying, to some degree, his earlier assertion that for the new nature "Christ is all and in all" (Col 3:11).

A life of such abandonment and availability is characterized by a deep, upwelling joy. Our heart rings with song, it reverberates with gratitude, it throbs with thankfulness because we are filled with the unshakable awareness of being exactly where we were created to be, rooted and grounded in the love of God. That love, God's cruciform love for us and our response of self-abandoning love for God, thrusts us into our world to be the incarnation of love for others.

On precisely this note Paul closes his exhortation to discipleship: "And whatever you do, in word or deed, do everything in the name of the Lord Jesus, giving thanks to God the Father through him" (Col 3:17 NRSV). Clearly Paul is pointing us to a mode of being in the world, not merely to modifications of behavior. Every activity of life is to be engaged "in the name of the Lord Jesus." What does this mean? The phrase seldomly appears in Paul's writings.[11] *Name,* however, has significant meaning in the context of Paul's Judaism. A name denoted the essence or core character of that which was named. On occasion, when persons experienced a transforming encounter with God, they received a new name, representative of their new nature.[12] In addition, to do something "in the name of" another was to represent the person named as if they were present and acting for him-or herself.[13] Thus to do something in the name of the Lord Jesus is to become the presence of Jesus doing the action, to do it in a manner that manifests Jesus' very nature. In the immediate context of putting on Christ (v. 14), letting the peace of Christ rule in our hearts (v. 15) and letting the word of Christ dwell in us richly (v. 16), and the more extended context of our life being hidden with Christ in God (v. 3) and Christ being our life (v. 4), Paul is calling us to a mode of being in which our false self has been crucified with Christ and no longer lives; rather Christ lives in us (Gal 2:19-20).

To do everything in the name of the Lord Jesus is to live our life in the world from a deep center of abiding in God. This is a life of radical abandonment to God in love and equally radical availability to God for others so that in all circumstances and relationships our life becomes one in whom God is present for others. The hallmark of such a life of abiding abandonment and availability is thankfulness—"giving thanks to God the

Father through him." Such thankfulness is not a perfunctory act of gratitude but a pervasive quality of being that results from having our being rooted in the love of God poured into our hearts through Christ.

It should be obvious by now that putting on the new nature is far more radical than attitude adjustments and behavior modifications. The life hidden with Christ in God is one of such growing union with God in love that God's presence becomes the context of our daily life, God's purposes become the matrix of our activities, and the values of God's kingdom shape our life and relationships; God's living presence becomes the ground of our identity, the source of our meaning, the seat of our value and the center of our purpose.

In chapter seven we will consider the spiritual practices that nurture this kind of life. However, here are some probes for your reflection on this chapter.

- What changes might take place in your life if you lived each moment in the conscious awareness that you are God's chosen one, holy and beloved?

- To what extent do compassion, kindness, lowliness, gentleness and patience characterize your relationships with others?
- What role does forbearance play in your relationships with others?
- Whom do you need to forgive? (Perhaps the most significant probe.)
- What cancerous root of bitterness and resentment is poisoning all your relationships?
- Do you have some idea of what "putting on Christ" might entail in your life?
- What would your life look like if the peace of Christ ruled in your heart?
- What would your life look like if the word of Christ dwelt in you richly?

You might take one hour seeking to do everything in the name of the Lord Jesus, giving thanks to God through him.

7

PRINCIPLES OF THE DEEPER LIFE

O holy Mystery, you who entered into the depths of my brokenness that I might be filled with your fullness, enflame my heart with your indwelling love that I might desire you above all else. May my growing love for you lead me to offer myself to you through practices of devotion and service. Through these practices may the light of your cruciform love break the power of the persistent shadows of my false self. May your light illuminate my darkness. May your cruciform love consume all evil in me. May your wholeness heal my brokenness and make me a child of light. This I pray in and through Christ Jesus our Lord, who lives and reigns with you and the Holy Spirit, one God, world without end. Amen.

The spiritual principles of the life that seeks loving union with God have two inseparable dimensions. One is our life of personal intimacy with God; the other is our life of public intimacy with God. These are neither either-or nor both/and options; they are an inseparable unity. These two dimensions might be imaged as a Möbius strip. Take a strip of paper about an inch wide and a foot long. Hold the two ends between your thumbs and forefingers with your thumbs on top. Bring the two ends together but twist the end in your right hand 180 degrees away from you so that the thumb side of the right end of the strip is on top. Tape or glue the ends of the strip together in this position. Now you have a strip with only one side! You know there are two sides to the strip, but as you trace a line around the strip you discover that there is now only one side. This is an illustration of the unity of the dimensions of personal and public intimacy with God. The two are one.

Remember the image of our life as a pipe open at both ends from chapter four (p. 94)? This pipe is created to be filled with God's presence. The filling, however, is not a static containment of God but a dynamic movement of God into and through us to the world. The filling comes as we grow to be persons through whom God becomes manifest in the world. One end of our pipe is designed for union with God in love (personal intimacy with God); the other end is for union with others in loving service (public intimacy with God). Only when both ends of the pipe are connected can the pipe be filled with the fullness of God's presence in us for others.

What are the principles that will nurture us in the dimensions of personal and public intimacy with God, an intimacy of loving union that will allow God to live in us for others and us to live in God for others? I use *principles* here rather than *practices* because spiritual practices will vary from person to person and from culture to culture. However, such practices, if they are to be effective in nurturing abandonment to God in love and availability to God for others, must be the implementation of certain essential principles of the deeper spiritual life.

PRACTICES OF PERSONAL INTIMACY WITH GOD

Personal intimacy with God is attentive to our inner life with God. Now the idea of an inner life with God is difficult for our false self, even our religious false self. Remember, our false self is a mode of being over against all that is not us, including God. Thus we usually posit God as a being outside of us. Consequently, our relationship with God is conceived as a relationship of two separate and autonomous beings who have decided to relate to one another in some manner. In this perspective, since God is usually conceived as a superior being of infinite characteristics, we come into the relationship as inferiors who must by some means attract, win and hold God's attention and favor. This is what the Colossians were trying to do with their lists of dos and don'ts, their rigorous religiosity, their false humility, their extreme ascetic practices (Col 2:21-23).

As Paul made abundantly clear, this approach to relationship with God is of no value at all.

The inner life with God is not something that we have to win, construct or engender. In a profound mystery God already dwells in the depths of our being in cruciform love. Augustine illustrates this reality with power and clarity:

> Too late loved I Thee, O Thou Beauty of ancient days, yet ever new! Too late I loved Thee! And behold, *Thou wert within,* and I abroad, and there I searched for Thee, deformed I, plunging amid those fair forms, which Thou hadst made. *Thou wert within me,* but I was not with Thee.[1]

Augustine, like us, sought for an external God, a God separate from himself. He discovered, however, that God is to be found and loved within the depths of our being. This is what Paul was pointing us to with his affirmation: "Your life is hidden with Christ in God" (Col 3:3 NRSV). It is to this presence of God in the depths of our being that we must be attentive, for it is here where loving union with God is engendered.

As persons who are habituated to a pervasive structure of self-referenced being, steeped in a radically decentered mode of being, we are mostly unaware of the deep inner dimensions of our life. To be sure, we have some awareness of psychology's perspective of the subconscious and unconscious dimensions of our self. However we are largely unaware of the deep spiritual ground of our being.

The frenetic busyness, attractions and diversions of our world draw us out of the deep center of our being and spread us thinly across the surface of our life. We are assaulted every waking moment by an incessant barrage of visual, aural and physical stimuli that compete for our attention and entice or demand our loyalty. Multiple media assail us with images, pictures and perceptions that subtly shape our understanding of our world and our place in it. Diverse value systems compete for our allegiance. Our lives become fragmented, our focus distorted, our minds and emotions a maelstrom of swirling and clashing currents. Thomas Merton describes well this state of existence:

> For as long as we live in our exterior consciousness alone, and identify ourselves completely with the superficial and transient side of our existence, then we are completely immersed in unreality. And to cling with passion to a state of unreality is the root of all sin: technically known as pride. It is the affirmation of our non-being as the ultimate reality for which we live, as against the being and truth of God. Hence we must become detached from the unreality that is in us in order to be united to the reality that lies deeper within and is our true self—our inmost self-in-God.[2]

Our greatest need then is to return to the deep center of our being, where God's very self is present to us in cruciform love as our true being.

Detachment and centering. There are two essential spiritual principles involved in this return to the center: detachment and centering.[3] Here too we are not dealing with a sequence of principles—first detachment and then centering—but a concurrent movement of our being from all that is not God to God as the center, source and content of our life. If we were to attempt to first detach ourselves from all that is not God in order to center ourselves in God we would quickly fall into the self-referenced activities of our religious false self. Detachment and centering are the crucial rhythms of the movement toward loving union with God. They are acts of devoted love for God. Any other motives for detachment and centering are ultimately expressions of self-referenced love.

Consequently, our times of personal aloneness with God must include practices of examining the not-God things into which the roots of our identity, meaning, value and purpose have been sunk. This does not necessarily mean things that are evil. Usually we have sunk the roots of our identity into things that, in and of themselves, are part of God's good creation, yet they are things that are never sufficient ground for our identity.

Simply identifying these false foundations of our identity is not sufficient. In order to detach our identity from those things we must yield ourselves to God in love precisely at those points of attachment.

There is an interesting feature in Jesus' dialogue with Peter in John 21:15-22. This is the account of Jesus' resurrection appearance to Peter and the disciples, who had been fishing all night but had caught nothing. After directing the disciples to a large catch of fish and preparing breakfast for them, Jesus then asks Peter, "Simon son of John, do you love me more than these?" (v. 15 NRSV). What is interesting here is that the antecedent for *these* is unstated and ambiguous. Is Jesus referring to the other disciples? Is he pointing to the large catch of fish, which would bring in a considerable amount of money? Is he indicating Peter's fishing equipment: the boat, nets, oars and sails? Or is Jesus alluding to the breakfast he has provided? It seems possible that the ambiguity is intentional. If there is anything Peter loves more than Jesus, then the nature of his relationship with Jesus is suspect.

This holds true for us. As we reflect on the things into which we have sunk some of the roots of our identity, we should hear Jesus saying, "Do you love me more than these?" The answer that leads to loving union with God in Christ is not a rational or cognitive one, but the deep movement of our hearts to God in love precisely at the point of that attachment.

One possible means for such detachment and centering would be to spend time daily reflecting with God around the prayer "Lord, free me from care for myself..." Let the Holy Spirit probe the activities, the relationships, the habits of head and heart that shape your life. Do you find manipulative, controlling dynamics in relating to others and the situations of your life? Are these reflective of the attachments of a self-referenced life? Do you find indulgences that have become debilitating prisons? Are these proof of the deep rooting of the selfreferenced life in something other than God? Do you find abusive, dehumanizing behaviors that demean and diminish others? Are these symptoms of the protectiveness and defensiveness of a self-referenced life? Do you find poisonous reservoirs of bitterness, resentment and hurt staining your relationships? Are these evidences of the unforgiveness of a self-referenced life?

As God's Spirit probes such areas of your life, the rest of the reflective prayer is "help me to have you as the sole content of my life today." Here is the movement where detachment segues to centeredness. At those points of manipulation, control, indulgence, abusiveness, bitterness and resentment, you offer your false self to God in loving abandonment. This inner movement of the heart toward God at the center must then be incarnated in those relationships and situations of the day where the behaviors of the self-referenced life have previously manifested themselves. Disciplines of loving abandonment to God right at the point of the old behaviors actualize the detachment and centering to which we committed ourselves in our time of aloneness with God. Where we have been manipulative and controlling of others, we offer the discipline of humility, seeking to work with others for the best interests of all, not merely our agenda. Where we have been indulgent, we offer the discipline of abstinence or simplicity. Where we have been abusive, we offer the discipline of compassion and kindness. Where we have been filled with bitterness and resentment, we offer the cruciform discipline of forgiveness.

Another movement of detachment and centering is also necessary if we are to be drawn into loving union with God. This is the movement of stilling ourselves in God and letting God be who God will be, and allowing God to do what God will do in and through us. The most marvelous biblical illustration of this is Psalm 131:

O Lord, my heart is not proud nor haughty my eyes;
I have not gone after things too great nor marvels beyond me.
Truly, I have set my soul in silence and in peace,

Like a weaned child at its mother's breast. *(The Abbey Psalter)*

I doubt that any of us can pray this prayer with integrity. Our hearts *are* proud; we constantly play god in our lives and in the lives of others. Our eyes *are* haughty; we regularly position ourselves above others. We *have* gone after things too great and marvels beyond us, trying to construct the world according to our own agenda. Consequently, we *rarely* set our souls in silence and peace. We *rarely if ever* become like a weaned child at its mother's breast—resting in an abandonment of love, not desiring the milk but content to simply be enfolded in love.

This psalm can also be used meditatively and lead us into contemplation—the posture of the weaned child at its mother's breast—deep centeredness and the heart of loving union with God. We can begin, "O Lord, let not my heart be proud" and then allow the Spirit to lead us to meditate on those aspects of our life in which we still play god, those areas where our will, our purpose, our desires rule our life and relationships. We then commit ourselves to the appropriate disciplines of detachment from those areas and of centering in God. We can then move to "nor haughty my eyes" and again allow the Spirit to probe the inner dynamics of our relationships with others where anything other than compassion, kindness, lowliness, gentleness and patience shapes those relationships. Again we commit ourselves to the appropriate disciplines of detachment and centering. Third, our prayer "Let me not go after things too great nor marvels beyond me" may allow us to reflect on Jesus' word, "Without me you can do nothing" (Jn 15:5), the last saying of Jesus our false self will ever acknowledge. Reflecting thus on our nothingness before God leads us finally to "Truly, help me set my soul in silence and in peace, like a weaned child at its mother's breast." We then seek to still the noise of our false self, withdraw with the mind into the heart and simply be in God's presence and love. Writing of how this life of loving union with God can be nurtured, Thomas Kelly says:

> By quiet, persistent practice in turning of all our being, day and night, in prayer and inward worship and surrender, toward Him who calls in the deeps of our souls. Mental habits of inward orientation must be established. An inner, secret turning to God can be made fairly steady, after weeks and months and years of practice and lapses and failures and returns.[4]

This "quiet, persistent practice" begins in the action of becoming a weaned child at our mother's breast in the daily times of aloneness with God. As that deep offering of our self to God in love begins to become habituated in our relationship with God, that centeredness begins to infuse our life outside the times of aloneness with God. Loving union with God, the life hidden with God in Christ, begins to become the reality of our life in the world in all relationships and situations. Gradually, probably without our awareness, God works a transformation within us so that our heart really becomes less proud, our eyes less haughty, and we rely less and less on our abilities and resources for being God's person in the world.

It must be emphasized here that this movement of detachment and centeredness is not a flight from the world. Such a false asceticism is merely another means by which our religious false self identifies us over against the world. The detachment and centeredness that is at the heart of a life of loving union with God is never a world-denying spirituality. It is only the detachment from our manipulative and possessive abuse of the world that enables the world to be the place of life with God, and our centering enables our lives to be in the world all that God has created them to be. Paul gives us a tremendous insight into this reality. Writing to Timothy of persons who apparently are engaged in a rigorous asceticism, Paul says:

> They forbid marriage and demand abstinence from foods, which God created to be received with thanksgiving by those who believe and know the truth. For

everything created by God is good, and nothing is to be rejected, provided it is received with thanksgiving; for it is sanctified by God's word and by prayer. (1 Tim 4:3-5 NRSV)

Paul appears to be dealing with a form of world-negating asceticism often manifested throughout the history of Christian spirituality. Such spirituality is characterized more by what it is not (not of the world) than what it should be (a life in which God is present to and for the world). Note Paul's antidote: "Nothing is to be rejected, provided it is received with thanksgiving; for it is sanctified by God's word and by prayer." Thanksgiving is the hallmark of a life abandoned to God in love. When our life is hidden with Christ in God, the entire creation becomes the arena in which Christ becomes manifest in and through us. All things become the context of our life of loving union with God, and thankfulness is that deep inner posture of our heart abandoned in love, which enables us to receive all things as God purposes them to be. All things become sanctified by the word of God; that is, they are restored to what God purposes them to be in our life, and they are sanctified by prayer, that is, by our engaging them with thankfulness out of a heart abandoned to God in love.

Instead of a world-denying asceticism, the movement of detachment and centering is ultimately world affirming. It restores us to our true and rightful relationship with the world and restores the world to its true and rightful place in God's purposes for our life in loving union with God for others. Detachment and centering not only restore us in our relationship with God as the source and content of our true life, they also restore us to the place and role we were created to have in the world.

Perhaps the essential movement of detachment and centering is most powerfully stated by Thomas Kelly:

We are torn loose from earthly a t t a c h m e n t s a n d ambitions—*contemptus mundi*. And we are quickened to a divine but painful concern for the world—*amor mundi*. He plucks the world out of our hearts, loosening the chains of attachment. And He hurls the world into our hearts, where we and He together carry it in infinitely tender love.[5]

This brings us to the other principle of loving union with God: public intimacy with God.

PRACTICES OF PUBLIC INTIMACY WITH GOD

Public intimacy with God focuses on our life with God in the world. In chapter three we noted the crucial distinction between "being in the world for God" and "being in God for the world". Public intimacy with God is being in God for the world. Once again Thomas Kelly succinctly describes this reality:

Now out from such a holy Center come the commissions of life. Our fellowship with God [personal intimacy with God] issues in world-concern. We cannot keep the love of God to ourselves. It spills over. It quickens us. It makes us see the world's needs anew. We love people and we grieve to see them blind when they might be seeing, asleep with all the world's comforts when they ought to be awake and living sacrificially, accepting the world's goods as their right when they really hold them only in a temporary trust. It is because from this holy Center we relove people, relove our neighbors as ourselves, that we are bestirred to be means of their awakening.[6]

One of the greatest dangers of personal intimacy with God is that the disciplines by which we offer our self to God in the activities and relationships of our daily life can be nothing more than self-referenced efforts at detachment from the destructive and debilitating dynamics of our false self. The inseparable "other side" of those disciplines is that they not only become a means of grace to detach us from our false self, they also become offerings of our self to God for others. The discipline by which we abandon our manipulative ways with others and situations can at the same time be a discipline of becoming available to God for them. The discipline by which we forgive those who have hurt, wronged and abused us may, in God's grace, become a discipline through which we are reconciled to them and become the means of their reconciliation to God.

There are, however, principles for public intimacy with God. Two essential principles can be illustrated and implemented through an incarnational praying of the Lord's Prayer,[7] first, incarnating the prayer "Our Father in heaven," and second, incarnating the prayer "Let your name be hallowed, let your kingdom come, let your will be done on earth as in heaven."

Our Father in heaven. Jesus teaches us to pray, "Our Father in heaven" (Mt 6:9 NRSV). This phrase can become one of the primary and essential facets of our public intimacy with God, being in God for the world. The first word, _our,_ indicates that as we initiate openness to God in prayer we don't do it in privatized isolation. We come to God within the matrix of all the relationships of our life, real and potential, close and most distant, regular and occasional. We come to God in the context of our life in human community, in both the broadest and in the narrowest sense. The entire human family is caught up in "our," as well as the closer web of our daily relationships and the closest network of friends and family. In the word *our,* our relationship with God and our relationships with others are inseparably intertwined. Our personal intimacy with God becomes inextricably intertwined with our public intimacy with God.

When we pray "Our *Father*" with integrity, the context of all our human relationships is transformed. Every person encompassed by *our* becomes beloved by God and becomes our sister and brother. Others are no longer valued for the ways they enhance our agenda or devalued for the ways they thwart our purposes. Others can no longer be pawns in our game, objects for the fulfillment of our desires or enemies to be demonized and destroyed. Every person becomes one whom God loves and for whom God's grace is constantly outpoured. Others are those for whom we are to be the sister or brother in whom God's love and grace touches them. "Our Father" instantly bonds us with God on the one hand and with others on the other. If we take these two words, *Our Father,* into our daily life, if we make them the subtext of every relationship, a prayer we breathe steadily behind the scenes of every relationship, our personal intimacy with God will become public intimacy with God in the matrix of our relationships. As we are engaged in any relationship, while talking and listening, while interacting with another, we can, at a deeper level, be constantly affirming "Our Father ... Our Father..."

When we pray "Our Father *in heaven*" with integrity, all of life is grounded in a radically alternative mode of being. *In heaven* is not a statement of location, it is the affirmation of God's realm of being in which every "our" can find wholeness of life in loving union with God in relationships with others. *In heaven* affirms a realm whose values, perspectives and practices are contrary to those of the pervasively self-referenced structures of our culture; a realm which, as Jesus said, is already in our midst (Lk 17:21). *In heaven* grounds all our relationships in the deeper reality of God's presence and God's purposes for individual and social wholeness. If we take these four words, "Our Father in heaven," out into our life, if we make them the subtext of every relationship, the reality of God's realm of shalom and justice will begin to become incarnate in us; public intimacy with God will become the ground of all relationships.

The first principle of public intimacy with God, therefore, is engaging every relationship of our life in the context of God's presence and transforming activity; it is incarnating the prayer "Our Father in heaven." The second principle emerges from the next series in the Lord's Prayer.

Let your name be hallowed. Jesus teaches us to pray, "Let your name be hallowed, let your kingdom come, let your will be done on earth as in heaven" (Mt 6:9-10). This is not the usual form in which we pray the Lord's Prayer, but it is closer to the Greek form that Matthew and Luke convey to us.[8] Our usual way of praying this portion is: "Hallowed be your name.

Your kingdom come. Your will be done"
(NRSV). The first element simply is a
statement of fact; the last two are
requests for God to implement God's
kingdom and will. The third-person
imperative, however, "let [something]
be done" carries an implication for the
one making the request or the one to
whom the request is being made.
Perhaps this can be illustrated from two
verses in Colossians we have worked
with above (Col 3:15-16). There Paul
says, "Let the peace of Christ rule in
your hearts.... Let the word of Christ
dwell in you richly" (NRSV). Now the
peace of Christ and the word of Christ
are realities totally beyond the
capabilities of the Colossians (or us) to
create or implement. These are realities
that can only be enacted through the
presence and action of Christ. But it is
abundantly clear that these realities will
not—indeed, cannot—be enacted in our
lives without our full and total openness,
receptivity and responsiveness to
Christ's presence and work in us. In
other words, we are implicitly essential
to the fulfillment of the injunction.

This is also true in these three elements of the Lord's Prayer. When we pray "Let your name be hallowed," we are not spectators sitting on the sidelines of life cheering for God to get into the game. This prayer is a radical commitment to live our lives in the world—"on earth"—in such a manner that something of God's very presence and nature can become manifest in and through us. We are acknowledging that we cannot, of our own ability, bring this about, but we are willing to live in such loving abandonment to God in all the situations of our daily life that God, the Word, might become flesh in us.

This is what Paul was pointing us toward in Colossians 3:17, where he exhorts us, "And whatever you do, in word or deed, do everything in the name of the Lord Jesus, giving thanks to God the Father through him" (NRSV). As we noted in our discussion of this passage, to act "in the name of Jesus" is to live in the world in the same relationship of loving abandonment to God that Jesus lived. This is a life of radical abandonment to God in love and equally radical availability to God for others so that in all circumstances and relationships our life becomes one in whom God is present for others. This is the life "hidden with Christ in God" (Col 3:3). Whenever we allow this Christ life to become manifest in our living, then, as Paul indicated, our life becomes a manifestation of Christlikeness. God's nature (name) becomes hallowed. We live in public intimacy with God by entering into each situation of our life with the prayer "Let your name be hallowed" framing all we are and do.

When we pray "Let your kingdom come," we aren't asking God to bring history to an end and whisk us to realms of glory, or to wave a magic wand and solve all the problems we face in our life. Rather, we are making a radical commitment to live our life in the world ("on earth") in such loving abandonment to God that the values and principles, the perspectives and dynamics of God's realm of life and wholeness become incarnate in and through our being and doing. Here too we are utterly incapable of actualizing the kingdom in this way. We can, however, through loving abandonment, allow God to incarnate kingdom life in and through us in the circumstances of our daily life.

To have "Let your kingdom come" as the driving force of our involvement in the circumstances of our daily life is to "strive for the things that are above, where Christ is, seated at the right hand of God" (Col 3:1). It is living in the world ("on earth") as a participant in an alternate reality. Such an alternative lifestyle is at the heart of Paul's injunction, "Let the peace of Christ rule in your hearts" (Col 3:15 NRSV). The peace of Christ is God's shalom, a realm of life and wholeness in loving union with God. To let the peace of Christ rule is to view every circumstance through the kingdom perspectives of love and justice, and to engage every circumstance with mercy and compassion. We live in public intimacy with God by living "Let your kingdom come" into each circumstance of every day.

When we pray "Let your will be done," we aren't seeking an arbitrary imposition of God's will on the events of our life or asking God to work things out right no matter what we do. Rather, we are making a radical commitment to live in such loving abandonment to God in the world ("on earth") that we might become an incarnation of God's will in our response to the events we experience. To have "Let your will be done" as the impetus for our involvement in the events of our life is to orient our whole being toward the things above where Christ is (Col 3:2). Our life is no longer our own; it is at God's disposal. Paul points to this when he exhorts us to "let the word of Christ dwell in you richly" (Col 3:16 NRSV). Paul seems to be indicating that we are to be thoroughly Christ-referenced. The very presence of Christ indwelling us in the depths of our being is to be the primal reality of our life as we live in Christ in every event of our daily life. We are to *be* the will of God in every event, not simply *do* the will of God. *Doing* God's will without *being* God's will quickly becomes legalism. *Being* God's will is impossible without *doing* God's will. We live in public intimacy with God by living "Let your will be done" into each event of every day, abandoning our self in love to God to be God's will in and through whom God's will is done on earth as in heaven.

Such incarnation of the Lord's Prayer, such public intimacy with God, is profoundly countercultural and deeply contrary to the structures and dynamics of our false self. Our false self and its world, even our religious false self, hallow position, power, prestige, possessions, popularity and performance. Identity, meaning, value and purpose are found in these. To live in public intimacy with God, to live so that God's name is hallowed, is to become lowly, powerless, without esteem, simple in lifestyle, unconcerned with the plaudits of the crowd, being in God for the world. Such a life becomes a threat to our false self and its world, especially to our religious false self. A God-hallowing life in such a world may come to manifest the ultimate revelation of God—cruciform love.

Our false self and its world, even our religious false self, is driven to actualize *our* agendas, to establish *our* kingdoms as the dominant reality. Our methods of manipulation, coercion, marginalization and control breed corruption, injustice, dehumanization of others, and destruction of humanity and its habitat. To live in public intimacy with God, to live so that God's kingdom comes, is to stand against the world's methods, and bring cleansing and healing to its results. Public intimacy with God does not become merely an alternative method of manipulation, coercion, marginalization and control (all characteristics of the religious false self) but an incarnation of God's shalom in which individuals and communities are valued, systemic evil is challenged by kingdom values, the marginalized are received and respected as part of the *our* of "Our Father," the voice of the disenfranchised is heard, the cycles of poverty are broken. Such kingdom living is a terrible threat to the status quo of our false self and its world, even to our religious false self with its social-action programs. Kingdom living subverts our false self and its world and thus may well incur the wrath that could result in its crucifixion.

Public intimacy with God is to *become* the will of God in a world of false selves, which seek only their own will, even labeling it "the will of God." Allowing God to be God on God's terms in our life in a world where self alone is god becomes a sign and threat to the very essence of the false self and its world. If the false self is not God, as it believes itself to be, then the entire structure of its life and world is undone. It is one thing to challenge the false self and its world's focus on position, power, prestige, possessions, popularity and performance as the ground of identity, meaning, value and purpose; to confront its methods of manipulation, coercion, marginalization and control and their destructive consequences; but it is quite another matter to attack the very heart of the false self and its world. This is why Jesus' bottom line as he stands in the shadow of crucifixion is "Your will be done" (Mt 26:42 NRSV).

The cross is the primal revelation of how our false self and its world responds to one who becomes the will of God in a world of false selves, to one who allows God to be God on God's terms. This reality lies at the heart of Jesus' call, "If any want to become my followers, let them deny themselves [i.e., abandon the false self] and take up their cross and follow me" (Mk 8:34 NRSV). Public intimacy with God, a life that becomes the will of God in a world that plays god, is a cruciform life, a life that moves against the very deepest current of the false self and its world.

THE DAILY OFFICE

If we are to engage the deeper journey into Christlikeness, if we are going to become more consistent in the integration of our personal and public intimacy with God, we must commit ourselves to a daily office. This term may be strange to you, or you may think of your Catholic friends, for whom the term is more common. This is, however, a term with a long history in the Christian spiritual tradition. In essence it refers to a daily disciplined time with God. It is more than this. It is the primary priority of our life if we are going to progress on the deeper journey. Jesus told us, "Seek first the kingdom of God, and everything else will fall into place" (Mt 6:33). When our daily office is merely one more task in an already busy schedule, it most likely will become simply another activity of our religious false self. We will have a daily office when it is convenient and perhaps let it become the first thing to be dropped out if our day is too busy.

If we are serious about the deeper journey, then we will have our daily office as the center of our life. All else will be ordered around this crucial time with God. All the issues of our life will be brought into God's presence in this time and receive their proper priorities. Things that seemed to be terribly important may come to be seen as irrelevant. Things that seemed to be insignificant may come to a place of great significance. This time with God becomes the center out of which we enter into our life in the world. After steady observance of our daily office, it gradually becomes the living center of our life with God that we carry out into the world with all its turmoils, troubles and tensions. Our daily office is where our life hidden with Christ in God is deepened.

You may be thinking, *Well, but what do I do during this daily office?* I can't give you the ideal daily office, but I will suggest certain elements that should be an essential part of your daily office.

First, there should be a time of centering yourself in God's presence. Acknowledge God as the context of your very being and the content of your living. Perhaps a phrase such as "New every morning is your love, and all day long you are working for good in the world"[9] will help center you and your life in the reality of God's presence. You can reflect on the activities of the day, your responsibilities, your relationships, your decisions and place them in the context of God's presence with you and at work in you in all of these things.

Second, there should be a desire to have God as the primary reality of your life during this day. Here a phrase like "Stir up in me the desire to be yours in all things today" may begin a process of deep inner reorientation of your being to God as the center. You may meditate on what your day holds (or held) and seek to allow God to show you what your day would be like if you allow God to actually be the sole content of your life.

Third, there needs to be a time of probing your being and your doing before God. Perhaps the request "Free me from care for myself" will open you to God at those points of anxious care that may be hindering your personal and public intimacy with God. As God reveals to you where caring for yourself is more important than love for God, commit yourself to offering yourself to God in a discipline that will detach you from those things and center you in God. Perhaps there is some indulgence in your life that reflects an inordinate "care for yourself," something you love more than God. The discipline here would be abstinence or moderation. Every time during the day you find yourself acting out of care for self, you simply stop and say to God, "I love you more than this, and I offer myself to you by abstaining from this indulgence."

Fourth, there needs to be a time of abandonment of yourself to God. A prayer like "Help me to have you as the sole content of my life today" might serve to begin and to deepen the inner orientation of your being to God rather than to yourself, your agenda, your purpose, your desires. You might reflect on what your life will look like if this prayer becomes incarnate in your living today.

Fifth, time should be spent in the Word. Praying the psalms, using a lectionary to move you through the whole Bible, not simply to fulfill an assignment but for the Scripture to become a place of transforming encounter with God. Read slowly, sink down into the text, let it become the context of your life at that moment. Listen to what God may be saying to you in that passage. Reflect on how this Word might become incarnate in your life in the world. If you receive a strong word from God in the passage, meditate on how living that word will look in your life, and commit yourself to God to incarnate that word in your living.[10]

Sixth, you need to spend some time in silence with God. This is extremely difficult for us at first. Stilling the noise of our life, both the outer and inner noise, seems almost impossible when we begin. But with continued practice, we can learn to be still and become aware of God's presence in the silence. In fact, we discover that God *is* the silence. Inner silence is not a space where God comes to meet us. When we are still, we know God as God (Ps 46:10). We begin to discover that at the core of our being God is, and that God is our true life. In Paul's words we begin to discover our life "hidden with Christ in God" (Col 3:3). If we daily practice silence, if we simply be in God, we will discover, with time, that this deep inner reality of our being begins to pervade all of our life. We begin to discover the heart of the deeper journey—living in God for the world.

EPILOGUE

This, then, is the deeper journey. It is a journey into the unfathomable wholeness of a life in loving union with God, a life of inexpressible joy, a life of unshakable peace, a life of world-shaking power, a life of infectious integrity, a life of healing grace, a life of transforming love.

The deeper journey takes place, however, in a world of secular and religious false selves, in a noxious nexus of self-referencedness, which rejects God as God on God's terms. In such a context, the deeper journey is a growth into an increasingly radical abandonment to God in love and an ever deepening availability to God in love for others.

The deeper journey gradually detaches the roots of our identity from anything other than God and draws us into a life of pervasive Christ-centeredness, a life hidden with Christ in God for the sake of the world.

The deeper journey is a cruciform path from a pervasively selfreferenced life into a thoroughly Christ-referenced life, a life of cruciform love in the world, a Christlike life for others.

May you allow God, in Christ, through the Holy Spirit, to lead you on this deeper journey.

NOTES

Chapter One: The Goal

[1] See the discussion of glory in Chapter 1.

[2] Archbishop Demetrios, "Voices from the Past Addressing Our Present," *Harvard Divinity Bulletin 30, no.4 (2002): 13 (emphasis added).*

[3] Athanasius *De Incarnatione* 54. (Athanasius lived in the A.D.300s.)

[4] Simeon the New Theologian *Catechesis* 22, lines 88-100.

[5] Gregory Palamas *Triads* 2.3.31, ed. John Meyendorff, trans. Nicholas Gendle, Classics of Western Spirituality (New York: Paulist Press, 1983).

[6] Bonaventura, *Legenda Maior* 9.1-2, in *The Life of St. Francis,* trans. Ewert Cousins, Classics of Western Spirituality (New York: Paulist Press, 1979).

[7] John of the Cross, *John of the Cross: Selected Writings,* ed.

Kieran Kavanaugh, Classics of Western Spirituality (New York: Paulist Press, 1987), p.235.

[8]   Ibid., p.257.

[9]   Teresa of Ávila *The Interior Castle* 2:3, trans. Kieran Kavanaugh and Otillo Rodriguez, Classics of Western Spirituality (New York: Paulist Press, 1979).

[10] Kallistos Ware, "The Eastern Tradition from the Tenth to the Twentieth Century," in *The Study of Spirituality,* ed. Cheslyn Jones, Geoffrey Wainwright and Edward Yarnold (New York: Oxford University Press, 1986), p.246.

[11] Kallistos Ware loc. cit. 254(emphasis added).

[12] Thomas Merton, "The Inner Experience: Christian Contemplation (III)," *Cistercian Studies Quarterly* 18 (1983): 210.

[13] John of the Cross, "The Living Flame of Love," prologue §1, in *John of the Cross: Selected Writings,* ed. Kieran Kavanaugh, Classics of Western Spirituality

(New York: Paulist Press, 1987), p.292.

Chapter Two: Into the Jungle

[1] *Self* is used here not in the contemporary sense of the psychological "self," an implicitly reductionistic term, but in the larger biblical sense of personhood framed within the context of a life lived in relationship with God, in community with others and as part of creation.

[2] I use *self-referenced* throughout to describe a way of being in the world with others that has grounded its identity, meaning, value and purpose in a matrix of relationships, activities and things in which God has no meaningful role.

[3] The term "false self" has a long history in Christian tradition beginning, as we will see (*infra.* 106), with the apostle Paul (Col 3:9) and finding its

contemporary use by such writers as Thomas Merton (see particularly *The New Man),* Basil Pennington *(True Self/False Self: Unmasking the Spirit Within),* Richard Rohr and David Benner.

[4] Gen 15:1; 21:17; 26:24; 46:3; Mt 14:27; 28:5; 28:10; Rev 1:17 to note a few.

[5] John Sharpe, "G.K. Chesterton's *Outline of Sanity,*" Houston *Catholic Worker* 22, no.7 (2002): 4.

[6] The usual translation is something like "for the mind that is set on the flesh," but the word that Paul uses for "the mind" is a word that deals with the deep inner posture of one's being.

Chapter Three: The Idol in the Box

[1] The March 13 reading of Oswald Chambers's *My Utmost for His Highest* (Menlo Park., Calif.: Willow Road Software, 1999).

[2] I will use "God" from here on to represent the construct we identify as God when we try to bring God into our life on our terms. While this construct may have affinities with God, it becomes an idol whenever we determine the boundaries of the relationship.

[3] Thomas A. Carlson, "Postmetaphysical Theology," in *Postmodern Theology,* ed. Kevin J. Vanhoozer (Cambridge: Cambridge University Press, 2003), p.60.

[4] The power of Paul's imagery is heightened when we realize that dogs were unclean animals for the Jews. A dog's droppings doubly so.

[5] I will provide "dynamic equivalence" translations of the Greek text of Colossians. Dynamic equivalence attempts to reproduce in contemporary terms and concepts the essence of the original text.

[6] Again, utilizing dynamic equivalence for translation.

[7]   This is a rather wooden translation of the Greek. The enigmatic nature of the phrase has led to a variety of translations that fail to grasp what Paul is saying.

Chapter Four: Hidden with Christ in God

[1]   See chapter one for a fuller development of this theme.

[2]   1 Chron 23:31; 2 Chron 2:4; 8:13; 31:3; Ezra 3:5; Neh 10:33; Ps 81:3; Is 1:14; Ezek 45:17; Hos 2:11.

[3]   In Joseph's dream, he and his brothers—the patriarchs of the twelve tribes—are imaged as stars.

[4]   Some translations of Rev 13:8 indicate that the names of those in rebellion against God are not written from before the foundation of the world in the book of life of the Lamb who was slain. The Greek of the best and strongest manuscripts, however, is perfectly clear: Their

names are not written in the
book of the life of the Lamb who
was slain before the foundation
of the world.

[5] See the discussion of *glory* on
pp.14-15.

[6] The Greek text has "heirs *of* God
and heirs together *of* Christ"
(emphasis added).

[7] "Heirs of God," "heirs of Christ,"
does not indicate we "inherit"
something from God or Christ
but that God and Christ are
themselves our "inheritance." We
are to be restored in the image
of God, which is Christlikeness.

[8] Lk 22:20; Jn 13:2, 4; 21:20; 1
Cor 11:20, 25.

[9] There will be a much fuller
discussion of forgiveness and its
vital role in the deeper journey
toward Christlikeness in chapter
six.

[10] See chapter three.

[11] The Greek word is κοινωνία,
indicating a close, deep, interpersonal
partnership, union together.

[12] Paul uses a chiastic structure
here:

A—resurrection

B—suffering

B'—suffering (death)

A'—resurrection

[13] "We love because God first loved us" (1 Jn 4:19).

[14] See the discussion of 2 Cor 5:14-15 on p.63.

[15] The phrase "set the mind" here again represents the Greek term better translated "orient your inner being."

[16] Paul, of course, was referring to the veil Moses put over his face (2 Cor 3:13; see Ex 34:33-35), which, however, Paul sees as a sign of Israel's hardness against God (2 Cor 3:14-16), that is, a symbol of their separation from God.

[17] The next ten sets of quotes from Scripture are from the NRSV. The emphasis in each case has been added.

[18] The prayer is that we may have power to comprehend the breadth, length, height and depth, that is, to know the love of Christ which surpasses

knowledge. The phrases "to comprehend" and "to know" are in an appositional structure, meaning each is the explanation for the other.

[19]   Thomas Merton, "The Inner Experience: Christian Contemplation (III)," *Cistercian Studies Quarterly* 18 (1983): 207.

[20] In the Greek both Christ (ὁ Χριστὸς) and your life (ἡ ζωὴ ὑμῶν) are in the nominative case, indicating they are the subject of the sentence.

[21]   See the discussion of *glory* on pp.14-15.

[22]   Thomas Kelly, *A Testament of Devotion* (New York: HarperCollins, 1996), p.28.

[23]   Ibid., pp.5, 8.

Chapter Five: Abandoning the False Self

[1]   The February 2 entry of Henri Nouwen, *Bread for the Journey* (San Francisco: Harper, 1997).

[2]   Aelred Squire, *Asking the Fathers* (New York: Paulist Press, 1976), p.103.

[3]   See 1 Jn 2:9-11; 3:10-11, 14-15, 17; 4:7-8, 11-12, 16, 20-21; 5:2.

[4]   See chapter ten of M. Robert Mulholland Jr., *Invitation to a Journey* (Downers Grove, Ill.: InterVarsity Press, 1993).

[5]   The source of this saying is unknown, but it did not originate with the author.

[6]   1 Cor, 2 Cor, Eph, Col, 1 Tim, 2 Tim.

[7]   Thomas Merton, "The Inner Experience: Kinds of Contemplation (IV)," *Cistercian Studies Quarterly* 18 (1983): 299.

[8]   Thomas Merton, "The Inner Experience: Christian Contemplation (III)," *Cistercian Studies Quarterly* 18 (1983): 206.

Chapter Six: Putting On the New Nature

[1]   The Greek term Paul uses for "chosen" in Col 3:12 is the same as in Eph 1:4.

[2]   Henri Nouwen, in a lecture delivered at Scarrett-Bennett Center, Nashville, Tennessee, February 8, 1991.

[3]   This is clear in the fact that "forbearing" and "forgiving" are participles modifying the leading verb "put on" by providing the context in which the virtues are to be put on.

[4]   Lance Morrow, "The Quality of Mercy: A South African Psychologist Ponders Forgiveness," *Time,* January 27, 2003, p.60 (emphasis added).

[5]   Corrie ten Boom, with Jamie Buckingham, *Tramp for the Lord* (New York: Fleming H. Revell, 1974), pp.55-57.

[6]   "The word translated "put on" is the same word Paul uses in Col 3:12!

[7]   Thomas Merton, "The Inner Experience: Christian Contemplation (III)," *Cistercian Studies Quarterly* 18 (1983): 207.

[8] Some translations have "word of Christ" at Rom 10:17, but the Greek term there is ῥήματος Χριστοῦ, not ὁ λόγος τοῦ Χριστοῦ as in Col 3:16, and in the Romans passage it is related to proclamation: "Faith is from hearing; hearing through the proclamation of Christ."

[9]   This "knowledge" is ἐπίγνωσιν, experiential knowledge as distinct from mere cognitive knowledge.

[10]   *Glory* refers to the very nature of Christ. Thus "Christ in you, the hope of glory" points to the restoration of the believer to the wholeness of the image of Christ (cf. discussion of *glory* on pp.14-15).

[11]   See 1 Cor 5:4; 6:11; Eph 5:20; Col 3:17; 2 Thess 3:6.

[12]   Abram becomes Abraham (Gen 17:5); Jacob becomes Israel (Gen 32:28). See also the

naming of Hosea's children to illustrate God's relationship with Israel (Hos 1:3-4, 6, 8-9).

[13] See 1 Sam 25:5-9; Esther 2:22; 8:8; Mt 18:5, 20. Compare Jer 14:14-18 on the danger of misrepresentation.

Chapter Seven: Principles of the Deeper Life

[1] Augustine *Confessions* 10.38, in *An Anthology of Devotional Literature,* comp. Thomas S. Kepler (Grand Rapids: Baker, 1977), p.81 (emphasis added).

[2] Thomas Merton, "The Inner Experience: Infused Contemplation (V)," *Cistercian Studies Quarterly* 19 (1984): 76.

[3] See chapter five, pp.111-14, for more on detachment.

[4] Thomas Kelly, *A Testament of Devotion* (New York: HarperCollins, 1996), pp.11-12.

[5] Ibid., pp.19-20.

[6] Ibid.,p. 98.

[7] The following is developed from M. Robert Mulholland, "The Word

Became Text: The Nature of Spiritual Reading," in *The Pastor's Guide to Personal Spiritual Formation,* **ed. William Willimon et al.** (Kansas City: Beacon Hill, 2005). The first three paragraphs here have already been introduced in chapter five, pp.108-9.

[8] Matthew has all three injunctions (Mt 6:9-10); Luke only has the first two (Lk 11:2).

[9] You can also use "afternoon" or "evening," depending on the time of day you have your daily office.

[10] You might want to look at Thomas Merton, *Opening the Bible* (Collegeville, Minn: Liturgical Press, 1970) or M. Robert Mulholland Jr., *Shaped by the Word: The Role of Scripture in Spiritual Formation* (Nashville: Upper Room, 1985, 2000) for help in the spiritual reading of Scripture.

APPENDIX

FOR REFLECTION AND DISCUSSION

This study guide provides an opportunity to reflect on what you have read and to engage with others who have done the same. In preparation for discussion flip through the book and make note of your favorite passages. Perhaps you have already done this by marking certain sections of your book. Come prepared to share the passages that most deeply affected you. You can also discuss how you responded (or plan to respond) to these sections.

For directed questions and discussion suggestions, multiple shorter sessions and one longer single session are offered. The first guide is for a group that meets for seven sessions, one for each chapter. The second guide is for a group that meets only once to discuss the book as a whole. If you aren't planning to be part of a group discussion, either set of questions will work for individual reflection. It would be helpful to have a Bible on hand as you work your way through the session(s).

A SEVEN-SESSION DISCUSSION GUIDE TO THE DEEPER JOURNEY

SESSION ONE

CHAPTER 1: THE GOAL

If the group is comfortable with spoken prayers, have someone open your time together by reading the prayer found at the beginning of the chapter and inviting the Lord's presence into your discussion.

1. Why did you want to read this book? Does the idea of a "deeper journey" strike a chord with you? Why or why not?

2. Where are you on your walk with God? Are you a newcomer to Christ? Or have you been on the Christian journey for some time? If time permits, participants may want to briefly share their faith journeys up to this point.

3. When you hear or see the phrase "What Would Jesus Do?" what

does that mean to you? What do you think it means to be like Jesus? How can you be like Jesus?

4.   Read Jesus' prayer in John 17:20-23, where he indicates that the purpose of the Christian life is to be in loving union with God, and that the source of a loving union with God lies in God's unfathomable love for us. Name some ways you have experienced God's love.

5.   In 2 Corinthians 3:18, what does Paul mean when he says we are being changed from "one degree of glory to another" (NRSV)?

6.   "To be like Jesus ... is a matter of both 'being' and 'doing.' It is being in a relationship of loving union with God that manifests itself in Christlike living in the world." Define the phrase "loving union," perhaps using the analogy of a union between a husband and wife.

7.   After reading the testimonies of people who have experienced an ecstatic, loving union with God, what is your response?

Skepticism? Hope? Jealousy? Have you ever experienced a rapturous moment with God?

8. What do you think is meant by the phrase "prayer of the heart"? In 1 Thessalonians 5:16-18, what do you think Paul means when he advises the Thessalonians to "pray without ceasing" (NRSV)?

9. Do you live in "loving union" with God in your everyday life, or are you hungering for a deeper divine relationship?

10. What is your response to the warning that this deeper journey into a loving union with God may be difficult at first?

SESSION TWO

CHAPTER 2: INTO THE JUNGLE

If the group is comfortable with spoken prayers, have someone open your time together by reading the prayer found at the beginning of the chapter and inviting the Lord's presence into your discussion.

1. Read Jeremiah 17:5-10. What images come to mind? How does the "shrub in the desert" illustrate one of the fundamental ways of being human? How does the "tree planted by water" illustrate the other way of being human? Do you see yourself as a shrub or a tree? Explain.

2. Paul says in Romans 7:19, "For I do not do the good I want, but the evil I do not want is what I do" (NRSV). In the author's personal example of a "Romans 7 moment," his negative attitude and behavior was prompted by a frustrating situation that was out of his control. Have you experienced a "Romans 7 moment" recently?

3. How does Cain display his false self in the story of Cain and Abel found in Genesis 4:1-16?

4. The essence of the false self is when we identify our self in radical separation from God, others and creation. Throughout human history this false self has led to destructive behavior toward

others for political, economic, social or other purposes. What are the consequences of such behavior? Be as broad or specific as you like.

5. Fear is a distinguishing characteristic of the false self; we fear we might not be valued and so compensate by finding our identity in our performance—"I am what I do." In what ways do you find your value in what you do? In what other places or roles do you find your true identity and value?

6. A corollary of our false self's fear is protectiveness; our false self constructs attitudes, habits, relationships and modes of interacting with the world that define our identity and protect us from real or imagined threats. How is Cain's construction of a city in Genesis 4:17 an example of this? (See Cain's story under "The False Self in the Biblical Story" subhead in this chapter.) What do you do to protect yourself?

7. Possessiveness is another characteristic of the false self; we find our identity in our possessions and material security. How does the story of Ananias and Sapphira from Acts 5:1-11 illustrate this point?

8. The characteristics of fearfulness, protectiveness, possessiveness and manipulation are seen in individuals and also in collectives such as a neighborhood, local community, state, nation or church. What are some recent examples in the news of one of these collectives acting in a fearful, protective, possessive or manipulative way?

9. How does Paul describe the false self ("life according to the flesh") in Galatians 5:19-21 and Romans 8:7? What does Paul say about life in the Spirit versus life of the flesh in Romans 8:1-14 (NRSV)?

10. How has this chapter helped you identify and work toward abandoning your false self to God? Either read aloud or take some quiet time to reflect on the

prayer found at the end of the chapter.

SESSION THREE

CHAPTER 3: THE IDOL IN THE BOX

If the group is comfortable with spoken prayers, have someone open your time together by reading the prayer found at the beginning of the chapter and inviting the Lord's presence into your discussion.

1. Read Matthew 16:24-25. What does Jesus mean when he says "those who lose their life for my sake will find it" (NRSV)?

2. What is the difference between the religious false self (being in the world for God) and the true self (being in God for the world)?

3. How are the Pharisees in the New Testament an example of the religious false self?

4. What are some of the fears of the religious false self? What do we do in response to that fear?

5. Sometimes our religious false self hides its fear behind a wall of activity in a performance-oriented attempt to validate our identity; we attend numerous worship services, Bible studies, prayer meetings, accountability groups and the like to reassure ourselves that our religious identity is secure. How does this behavior affect our ability to develop a deeper relationship of loving union with God?

6. Since knowledge is power, how does the religious false self seek to acquire control? How does this become idolatrous?

7. How can the religious false self be destructive in a community of faith?

8. Read Philippians 3:7-9. How is Paul's testimony a vivid portrayal of the self-destructiveness of the religious false self?

9. Have you encountered people or churches who define the Christian life by abstinence from certain things, where their religion is shaped by that detachment rather

than by a loving attachment to God? When have you allowed yourself to be more defined by detachment than attachment?

10.   Read the questions regarding the motivations for reading this book found at the end of the chapter. Take some time to reflect on these questions individually or discuss them as a group.

SESSION FOUR

CHAPTER 4: HIDDEN WITH CHRIST IN GOD

If the group is comfortable with spoken prayers, have someone open your time together by reading the prayer found at the beginning of the chapter and inviting the Lord's presence into your discussion.

1.   Do you think of your life as being regularly immersed in blessing (as Paul states in Ephesians 1:3)? Name a time when you felt blessed and a time when you didn't.

  Read Philippians 4:4-6. Why is it difficult for us to heed Paul's command to "Rejoice in the Lord always" and "not worry about anything" (NRSV)?

3. "You are a beloved child of God.... The primary center of your identity is the heart of God's love before the foundation of the world." How do you respond to this truth? Hopeful? Doubtful? Awestruck? Humbled?

4. How does Jesus' death on the cross reveal the very essence of God's nature?

5. In Matthew 16:24, Jesus says, "If any want to become my followers, let them deny themselves and take up their cross and follow me" (NRSV). How does this relate to the abandonment of the false self?

6. What will God do when we open our doors and let him come into our false self?

7. What are some doors of the false self? What might be the door or doors in your life? Can you think of past examples from your life when you were able to open a

door and let go of your false self? Do you have a possessive or protective grip on any door?

8. What does Paul say about the reality of loving union with God in Ephesians 3:16-19?

9. When we live in loving union with God, our life becomes a place where others experience the presence of God's love, mercy and grace. Share a time when you were on the receiving end of this love, mercy and grace through someone you know.

10. Read the questions found in the conclusion of the chapter. Take some time to reflect on these questions individually or discuss them as a group.

SESSION FIVE

CHAPTER 5: ABANDONING THE FALSE SELF

If the group is comfortable with spoken prayers, have someone open your time together by reading the prayer found at the beginning of the

...pter and inviting the Lord's presence into your discussion.

1. Abandoning our false self can't take place in a vacuum; it must happen in the context of our relationships with others. What does Mark 12:30-31 say about this?

2. In Matthew 6:9, Jesus teaches us to pray, "Our Father in heaven." How does this connect our relationship with God to our relationships with others?

3. In Colossians 3:9-10, what two things does Paul indicate are required to avoid being false with others?

4. How is detachment from our false self possible?

5. As an exercise in detachment, fill in the following sentence: "Lord, help me to love you more than _____ (e.g., possessions, status, profession, performance, woundedness, etc.)." Write your answers on small slips of paper (do not include your name) and then gather the slips together, perhaps laying them at the foot

of a small cross. Pray and ask for the Lord's help in putting to death these markers of your false self.

6. Why can't we put on our new nature on our own? Why do we need God?

7. Paul tells us that in our new nature "there is no longer Greek and Jew, circumcised and uncircumcised, barbarian, Scythian, slave and free; but Christ is all and in all" (Col 3:11 NRSV). How does this affect our relationships with others who are different from us?

8. Colossians 3:11 concludes that "Christ is ... in all." What do you think this means?

9. How do the actions of Mother Teresa exemplify that Christ is in all?

10. Read the questions found in the conclusion of the chapter. Take some time to reflect on these questions individually or discuss them as a group.

SESSION SIX

CHAPTER 6: PUTTING ON THE NEW NATURE

If the group is comfortable with spoken prayers, have someone open your time together by reading the prayer found at the beginning of the chapter and inviting the Lord's presence into your discussion.

1. Paul addresses his readers as "God's chosen ones, holy and beloved" (Col 3:12). There is nothing we can do to make God love us more or to make him love us less. What does this mean to you? Is it difficult for you to believe that we are beloved no matter what we do? Why or why not?

2. What is holiness? What does it mean to be holy?

3. Read the list of virtues found in Colossians 3:12. How can you apply these virtues in your everyday life with others?

4. Which of these virtues—compassion, kindness, humility, meekness (or gentleness), patience—is difficult for you? Discuss these virtues in terms of the false self and the true self.

5. In Colossians 3:13, Paul tells us to "bear with one another" (NRSV). What does it mean for us to be forbearing with each other?

6. We are called to forgive unconditionally. What is unconditional forgiveness? Share a time when you have been forgiven unconditionally or when you have had to forgive someone unconditionally. If someone in the group is currently wrestling with unconditional forgiveness, take time to pray for that relationship.

7. Why is unconditional forgiveness impossible to do on our own? Why do we need God?

8. In order to put on a new nature, we need to put on Christ. What does this mean?

9. We are called into loving union not merely with God in Christ but also with our sisters and brothers. What does 1 John 4:20-21 say about that?

10. Read the questions found in the conclusion of the chapter. Take some time to reflect on these questions individually or discuss them as a group.

SESSION SEVEN

CHAPTER 7: PRINCIPLES OF THE DEEPER LIFE

If the group is comfortable with spoken prayers, have someone open your time together by reading the prayer found at the beginning of the chapter and inviting the Lord's presence into your discussion.

1. Why is union with others in loving service (public intimacy with God) equally as important as union with God in love (personal intimacy with God)?

2. Personal intimacy with God requires us to be attentive to our

inner life with God. How does daily prayer time help us with this?

3. What kinds of things should we be reflecting on during our times of personal aloneness with God? How are detachment and centering key to these times?

4. If time allows, have someone in the group lead you on the meditation practice suggested for Psalm 131 (found under the subhead "Detachment and centering").

5. What is the focus of public intimacy with God?

6. What principles for public intimacy with God are illustrated in the Lord's Prayer (Mt 6:9-14)?

7. How is the Lord's Prayer a radical commitment to live in the world (Mt 6:10)?

8. When we pray "Let your will be done," what does that mean?

9. Why should a daily office (i.e., a daily disciplined time with God) be the center of our life? What should be part of that daily office?

10. How has this book helped you understand the deeper journey? What lessons, principles or practices will help you grow in loving union with God and others?

A SINGLE-SESSION DISCUSSION GUIDE TO THE DEEPER JOURNEY

If the group is comfortable with spoken prayers, have someone open your time together by reading the prayer found at the beginning of chapter one and inviting the Lord's presence into your discussion.

1. Why did you want to read this book? What does the idea of a "deeper journey" convey to you? Is it appealing? Why or why not?

2. "To be like Jesus ... is a matter of both 'being' and 'doing.' It is being in a relationship of loving union with God that manifests itself in Christlike living in the world." Define the phrase "loving union," perhaps using the analogy of a union between a husband and wife (chap. 1).

3. Do you live in "loving union" with God in your everyday life, or are you hungering for a deeper divine relationship (chap. 1)?

4. The essence of the false self is when we identify our self in radical separation from God, others and creation. Throughout human history this false self has led to destructive behavior toward others for political, economic, social or other purposes. What are the consequences of such behavior? Be as broad or specific as you like (chap. 2).

5. Fear is a distinguishing characteristic of the false self; we fear we might not be valued and so compensate by finding our identity in our performance—"I am what I do." In what ways do you find your value in what you do (chap. 2)?

6. How has chapter two helped you identify and work toward abandoning your false self to God? Either read aloud or take some quiet time to reflect on the prayer found at the end of the chapter (chap. 2).

7. What is the difference between the religious false self (being in the world for God) and the true

self (being in God for the world) (chap. 3)?

8. What are some of the fears of the religious false self? What do we do in response to that fear (chap. 3)?

9. "You are a beloved child of God.... The primary center of your identity is the heart of God's love before the foundation of the world." How do you respond to this truth? Hopeful? Doubtful? Awestruck? Humbled (chap. 4)?

10. What are some doors of the false self? What might be the door or doors in your life? Can you think of past examples from your life when you were able to open a door and let go of your false self? Do you have a possessive or protective grip on any door (chap. 4)?

11. Abandoning our false self can't take place in a vacuum; it must happen in the context of our relationships with others. What does Mark 12:30-31 say about this (chap. 5)?

12. In Matthew 6:9, Jesus teaches us to pray, "Our Father in heaven." How does this connect our relationship with God to our relationships with others (chap. 5)?

13. Paul addresses his readers as "God's chosen ones, holy and beloved" (Col 3:12). There is nothing we can do to make God love us more or to make him love us less. What does this mean to you? Is it difficult for you to believe that we are beloved no matter what we do? Why or why not (chap. 6)? Read the list of virtues found in Colossians 3:12. How can you apply these virtues in your everyday life with others and how might their application be affected by the false self and the true self (chap. 6)?

14. Why is union with others in loving service (public intimacy with God) equally as important as union with God in love (personal intimacy with God) (chap. 7)?

15. What principles for public intimacy with God are illustrated in the Lord's Prayer (Mt 6:9-14) (chap. 7)?

16. Why should a daily office (i.e., a daily disciplined time with God) be the center of our life? What should be part of that daily office (chap. 7)?

17. How has this book helped you understand the deeper journey? What lessons, principles or practices will help you grow in loving union with God and others?

TITLES FROM M. ROBERT MULHOLLAND JR.

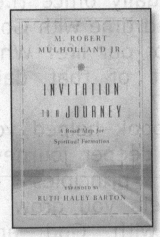

Invitation to a Journey

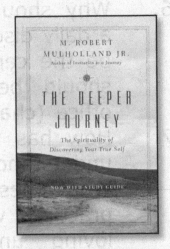

The Deeper Journey

*Spritual Transformation for
the Sake of Others DVD*

TRANSF**O**RMING CENTER
Strengthening the Soul of Your Leadership

The best thing you bring to leadership is your own transforming self!

The Transforming Center exists to strengthen the souls of pastors, Christian leaders, and the congregations and organizations they serve. Don't just learn about spiritual transformation—experience it in your own life!

Ruth Haley Barton (doctor of divinity, Northern Seminary) is founder of the Transforming Center.

Visit the Transforming Center online to learn more about:
- *Transforming Community*®: A two-year experience of spiritual formation for leaders

- Earning a doctor of ministry, a master's specialization or a certificate in spiritual transformation
- Regional and national events for pastors and ministry leaders
- Teaching and transformational experiences for your congregation
- *Transforming Church®:* A network of churches and leaders who affirm that spiritual transformation is central to the Gospel and therefore central to the mission of the church
- *Transforming Resources®:* Print and electronic tools to guide leaders and their communities in experiencing spiritual transformation

Join thousands of pastors and Christian leaders...

subscribe today to our free *eReflections,* spiritual guidance via email.

To subscribe, visit:
www.TransformingCenter.org

TRANSF◯RMINGRESOURCES
A Ministry of the Transforming Center®

Tools to guide leaders and their communities in experiencing spiritual transformation.

Beyond mere information, each resource is designed to provide step-by-step guidance for engaging the practices, experiences and relationships that foster greater intimacy with God and deeper levels of spiritual transformation.

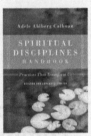

Strengthening the Soul of Your Leadership

Life Together in Christ

Pursuing God's Will Together

Spiritual Disciplines Handbook, Revised

Sacred Rhythms
Sacred Rhythms DVD curriculum

Invitation to Solitude and Silence

Longing for More

Invitations from God

To see the complete library of Transforming Resources, visit:
www.Resources.TransformingCenter.org

CPSIA information can be obtained
at www.ICGtesting.com
Printed in the USA
LVHW091625140722
723497LV00006B/355

9 780369 372598